Revolution in Education

AURORA AMORIS

REVOLUTION IN EDUCATION

The Future of Learning with AI

2025

Revolution in Education

Aurora Amoris

CONTENTS

CHAPTER 1

Artificial Intelligence in Education

1.1. The Role of AI in Education

Artificial intelligence is essentially reshaping education through growing new opportunities and challenges. In the area of education, AI is being hired to enhance personalized getting to know, enhance educational management, and transform conventional teaching strategies. Its integration into the study room, on line structures, and administrative systems marks the start of a extensive shift toward extra green, statistics-driven, and reachable training.

AI's potential to manner enormous quantities of information quick allows for the introduction of dynamic learning environments that can be tailored to the particular needs of college students. It can analyze patterns in pupil conduct, instructional performance, and mastering styles to create a greater individualized getting to know revel in. This generation also can streamline administrative obligations, which include grading, curriculum planning, and scheduling, enabling instructors and establishments to focus extra on delivering nice training.

Moreover, AI in education extends beyond the study room. Through sensible tutoring structures and digital learning equipment, it enables get right of entry to to know-how for a broader target audience, regardless of area or monetary historical past. In particular, on line publications, virtual school rooms, and AI-primarily based educational gear are breaking down the traditional limitations to education, supplying a extra inclusive and bendy approach to studying.

However, the substantial implementation of AI in training raises several moral and practical concerns. The series of student records, vital for AI structures to function effectively, provides great privacy and safety dangers. Additionally, there's the continuing debate approximately the role of AI in making educational choices, from grading assignments to figuring out scholar potential. These issues spotlight the need for careful law and oversight to make sure that AI's impact on schooling stays high quality and equitable.

As AI era keeps to evolve, its position in education will amplify, imparting new possibilities for boosting gaining knowledge of experiences while addressing the demanding situations that include those improvements.

1.2. AI and the Student Experience

Artificial intelligence is profoundly altering the scholar revel in, from personalised studying pathways to developing dynamic, interactive environments that foster deeper engagement with the fabric. AI enables instructional structures to evolve to the needs, choices, and mastering varieties of character students, thereby improving the overall experience and growing the effectiveness of gaining knowledge of.

The integration of AI into the instructional enjoy allows for greater tailored instruction. By analyzing a student's past overall performance, mastering pace, and behavioral statistics, AI can advocate assets, assignments, and sports that cater specifically to their desires. This level of customization guarantees that students can progress at their personal pace, spending greater time on subjects that require interest and transferring forward when they've mastered certain ideas. In this manner, AI no longer handiest helps gaining knowledge of but additionally actively complements it by using creating an revel in that is extra relevant and green for each scholar.

Moreover, AI has made sizable strides in supplying instantaneous feedback, some thing this is regularly lacking in traditional study room settings. With AI-powered structures, college students receive on the spot responses to their work, allowing them to address mistakes and misconceptions quickly. This continuous comments loop enhances mastering retention and facilitates college students live on course at some point of their instructional adventure.

In addition to personalized content, AI-pushed platforms additionally provide a extra interactive experience. Virtual lecture rooms and AI-powered tutoring systems can simulate one-on-one interactions, in which students can obtain guidance and support with out the limitations of time or location. Such platforms can also even encompass herbal language processing abilities, allowing students to ask questions in real-time and get hold of contextually applicable solutions, simulating the revel in of engaging with a human tutor.

However, whilst AI offers promising possibilities to decorate the scholar enjoy, it additionally raises questions about the capability loss of the human contact in schooling. The courting between college students and educators is often a key element of the learning procedure. With AI systems taking on a few elements of teaching, the query arises whether this may decrease the role of educators as mentors, motivators, and function fashions. The balance among automation and human interplay will need to be cautiously controlled to ensure that AI complements, rather than replaces, vital factors of the student revel in.

AI has the potential to revolutionize the pupil enjoy by way of presenting personalised, interactive, and adaptive learning environments. By offering immediately comments, tailoring practise to individual wishes, and growing bendy instructional pathways, AI empowers college students to take manipulate of their personal getting to know, enhancing each engagement and academic fulfillment. However, the mixing of AI into schooling ought to be treated thoughtfully, making sure that it enhances traditional educational values and maintains the human connection this is critical to holistic getting to know.

1.3. Technological Trends and Transformation

The rapid advancement of technology is essentially reshaping the panorama of schooling, and artificial intelligence is at the vanguard of this alteration. AI technologies are using new tendencies and improvements that project conventional instructional fashions and open up new possibilities for a way studying may be structured, introduced, and experienced. These technological shifts aren't only changing how training is carried out however are also influencing the wider societal knowledge of what getting to know and know-how acquisition must look like within the destiny.

One of the primary technological developments shaping the educational landscape is the shift towards customized mastering. AI's capacity to analyze great amounts of records and alter mastering content and methods primarily based on person desires has propelled customized gaining knowledge of into the mainstream. Adaptive mastering structures powered by using AI can tune a pupil's development and tailor training to their strengths and weaknesses. This flexibility permits for a extra pupil-targeted method, where novices have the liberty to develop at their own pace, get hold of focused interventions while vital, and interact with material in a way that suits their preferred getting to know patterns.

Another sizeable fashion is the increasing use of data analytics in schooling. AI structures can collect and examine facts from various assets, such as pupil performance, engagement levels, and behavioral styles. This records can be used to inform selection-making, improve coaching strategies, and predict getting to know consequences. Teachers and administrators can use those insights to perceive struggling college students early, personalize guidance, and make informed changes to curricula and teaching strategies. The capacity to harness data on this way offers unprecedented opportunities for continuous improvement and optimization inside educational structures.

Moreover, AI is driving the improvement of immersive learning stories, specifically thru the usage of digital and augmented reality (VR and AR). These technologies, when blended with AI, allow the creation of particularly attractive and interactive studying environments. Students can explore virtual worlds, have interaction with 3-D fashions, and have interaction in simulations that could be difficult or not possible to copy in conventional classroom settings. Such immersive reviews can deepen know-how, enhance retention, and provide college students with the capability to practice capabilities in a safe and managed surroundings.

AI's impact extends beyond the classroom to the worldwide education atmosphere, because it facilitates the increase of online mastering platforms and educational technology. The rise of Massive Open Online Courses (MOOCs), AI-powered learning control systems, and other virtual equipment has made training more on hand to people around the world. Students can now research from everywhere, at any time, and at their personal tempo, breaking down geographical and temporal boundaries. These innovations are transforming training right into a extra bendy and inclusive enterprise, permitting inexperienced persons from numerous backgrounds and places to take part in exquisite educational reviews.

However, these technological advancements also gift challenges and risks. The growing reliance on AI and records-driven decision-making increases concerns approximately privateness, safety, and the moral implications of using such powerful gear in training. As AI systems gather huge quantities of personal information approximately college students, making sure the protection of this information will become a essential priority. Additionally, as academic systems undertake AI, there is a want for ongoing evaluation of the era's effect on coaching, getting to know results, and societal equity.

The ongoing technological transformation in schooling is simple, with AI at the middle of this shift. As personalized gaining knowledge of, facts analytics, immersive technology, and international get entry to to education hold to conform, AI will play an an increasing number of large position in reshaping how information is delivered and skilled. However, the accountable implementation of these technologies is important to making sure that they advantage all students and educators, without compromising privacy or ethical requirements. The future of training, formed by way of AI and different technology, holds tremendous ability, but it ought to be carefully navigated to make sure that it serves the more top of society.

1.4. Historical Development of AI in Education

The integration of synthetic intelligence (AI) into education did now not arise all of sudden, nor did it emerge in a vacuum. It has been a slow method influenced through broader technological traits, theoretical improvements in computer technology, shifts in academic theory, and socio-monetary imperatives. The journey from the earliest ideas of gadget intelligence to today's wise tutoring structures and adaptive getting to know platforms represents no longer most effective the evolution of generation but also the converting perception of the way human beings research and how machines can help that studying.

The ancient improvement of AI in schooling can be traced via several distinct however overlapping stages: the theoretical foundations (1950s–1970s), the early experimental structures (1980s –1990s), the net revolution and the rise of smart tutoring systems (2000s), the emergence of large records and system studying programs (2010s), and the modern-day segment of integrated, scalable, and adaptive AI-powered training ecosystems (2020s onward). Each of these stages reflects broader shifts in each AI studies and academic priorities.

The conceptual basis for AI in training emerged along the wider field of synthetic intelligence. In the 1950s, pioneers consisting of Alan Turing and John McCarthy laid the theoretical foundations for system intelligence. Turing's well-known query—"Can machines assume?"—proposed in his seminal 1950 paper, Computing Machinery and Intelligence, not directly planted the seed for the usage of smart machines in cognitive domain names like mastering and teaching.

During the 1960s and 1970s, the dominant technique in AI studies was symbolic AI, or "excellent old style AI" (GOFAI). Researchers aimed to encode human information and reasoning into formal symbolic systems. In the context of education, this gave rise to early models of cognitive psychology that tried to simulate human notion and problem-fixing, which could later tell sensible tutoring systems (ITS).

One of the most influential early works throughout this era become the Socratic-fashion talk model, which attempted to imitate the way teachers manual college students via inquiry. Researchers realized that teaching turned into not pretty much turning in records however approximately carrying out cognitive approaches. The foundations of constructivist learning concept—championed by using scholars like Jean

Piaget and Seymour Papert—emphasised active learning, and Papert's paintings on Logo, a programming language designed for kids, symbolized one of the earliest intersections of laptop technological know-how, training, and AI.

Although the real computational potential of systems at some stage in this period became restrained, the philosophical and psychological basis laid the path for future integration.

The 1980s marked a turning factor with the development of the first generation of intelligent tutoring structures (ITS). These structures aimed to simulate the behavior of human tutors through adapting educational techniques to the desires of individual inexperienced persons. Unlike traditional laptop-assisted practise, which presented the identical content to all inexperienced persons, ITS integrated fashions of domain expertise, scholar know-how, and pedagogical techniques.

One of the pioneering systems was SOPHIE (Socratic Physics Tutor), evolved in the past due 1970s and early 1980s. SOPHIE could diagnose college students' misconceptions in electronics and guide them through problem-solving. Similarly, ANDES and AutoTutor emerged as remarkable ITS platforms in the 1990s. These structures used cognitive models to conform content and remarks to person rookies, simulating human-like coaching.

Another primary improvement during this era turned into constraint-based totally modeling, which allowed systems to evaluate scholar solutions no longer with the aid of matching predefined solutions however through identifying violations of conceptual constraints. This approach proved valuable in arithmetic and pc technological know-how education, where multiple correct answers regularly exist.

However, those structures faced demanding situations. They had been high-priced and time-ingesting to increase, commonly domain-unique, and hard to scale. Still, the research conducted at some stage in this time tested the potential of AI to guide mastering in state-of-the-art and personalised approaches.

Concurrently, the wider subject of schooling era noticed the upward push of pc-based totally training (CBT) programs, multimedia CD-ROMs, and the early use of gaining knowledge of management structures (LMS). Although not all of those were AI-pushed, they set the level for digital training environments in which AI might later flourish.

The proliferation of the internet inside the past due 1990s and early 2000s transformed educational delivery strategies. Online mastering environments became increasingly famous, and with them got here a developing hobby in personalization and statistics-pushed guidance. While early e-mastering platforms have been largely static and linear, researchers started out integrating AI strategies to create extra adaptive and responsive systems.

During this era, numerous vast developments befell:

• Carnegie Learning released Cognitive Tutor, one of the first industrial ITS merchandise that achieved sizeable adoption in U.S. Colleges. Based on years of cognitive technological know-how research at Carnegie Mellon University, it used rule-primarily based modeling to adapt to students' gaining knowledge of development in algebra and different subjects.

• AutoTutor, advanced on the University of Memphis, applied herbal language processing to simulate conversational interactions with college students. Unlike in advance ITS, which relied heavily on more than one-choice or structured responses, AutoTutor tried to interact rookies through talk.

• The emergence of Bayesian networks and probabilistic modeling allowed structures to handle uncertainty in scholar conduct and gaining knowledge of trajectories extra effectively. These strategies progressed the adaptability and realism of tutoring structures.

• AI-powered diagnostic exams commenced to appear, enabling structures to quick pick out a pupil's know-how nation and alter content material as a result. This become a shift from "one-size-suits-all" guidance to personalised getting to know paths.

Despite those improvements, massive-scale implementation remained restrained because of technological constraints, high improvement charges, and institutional inertia. Nonetheless, the basis changed into being laid for the subsequent phase of AI-driven training.

The 2010s were characterized by using an explosion in facts availability, advances in gadget learning algorithms, and the upward thrust of cloud computing. These traits drastically stronger the abilties of AI systems in schooling.

One of the maximum influential principles at some stage in this decade became studying analytics—the gathering, analysis, and interpretation of information about newcomers and their contexts. Learning analytics enabled instructional systems to display pupil engagement, are expecting overall performance, and customize content in actual-time. Combined with device studying, these structures began to approximate the adaptiveness and intuition of human instructors.

Adaptive gaining knowledge of structures such as Knewton, DreamBox, and Smart Sparrow emerged as pioneers in delivering personalised instruction at scale. These systems amassed sizable quantities of learner facts and used predictive modeling to adjust content material trouble, pacing, and sequencing. For example, DreamBox's math curriculum ought to adapt training primarily based on a infant's conduct, accuracy, or even hesitation patterns.

Massive Open Online Courses (MOOCs), which include the ones presented by using Coursera, edX, and Udacity, began incorporating AI factors like automated grading, content material advice, and discussion board moderation bots. Natural language processing enabled automated essay scoring and comments systems, whilst advice engines recommended publications or content material primarily based on learner conduct.

Voice recognition and digital assistants, inclusive of IBM Watson Tutor, started out to enter the instructional area, presenting shrewd question responses, customized help, and curriculum steering.

The growing use of AI also caused elevated interest on ethics, privateness, and bias. Concerns over scholar records use, surveillance, and algorithmic fairness have become important to the discourse surrounding AI in schooling.

The 2020s have witnessed the speedy acceleration of AI in schooling, catalyzed in element by means of the global COVID-19 pandemic, which pressured a huge shift closer to online and hybrid mastering. Educational establishments, edtech companies, and governments grew to become to AI-powered gear to manage remote studying, assist instructors, and engage college students.

Current AI applications encompass:

• AI chatbots utilized in universities for administrative responsibilities, instructional advising, or even basic tutoring.

• Multimodal studying analytics combining information from keystrokes, eye tracking, facial expression analysis, and more to create exact learner profiles.

- Generative AI equipment like GPT-based totally fashions are now used to guide innovative writing, programming assistance, and content material generation.

- AI tutors and co-pilots that offer just-in-time assistance at some point of lessons, checks, or mission work.

- Language getting to know systems which includes Duolingo have integrated deep gaining knowledge of fashions to tailor classes, speech popularity, and comments.

Today's AI systems are extra scalable, generalizable, and person-friendly than ever earlier than. The convergence of AI with augmented reality (AR), virtual fact (VR), and brain-computer interfaces promises a destiny of immersive, adaptive, and surprisingly customized getting to know studies.

Furthermore, the growing use of federated gaining knowledge of and privateness-preserving AI addresses some of the earlier worries approximately records protection and student privateness.

Governments and educational establishments have commenced adopting national AI in education strategies. For example, China's authorities has closely invested in AI-primarily based lecture rooms, at the same time as the European Union has emphasised ethical frameworks and responsible deployment.

The ancient development of AI in education exhibits not simply technological evolution however also a deepening information of pedagogy, human cognition, and social fairness. The journey from primitive rule-based totally tutors to these days's big language fashions embedded in getting to know management systems demonstrates how AI has matured from a theoretical possibility to a sensible necessity.

However, demanding situations stay: fairness of get admission to, ethical deployment, instructor training, and the avoidance of over-reliance on computerized systems. The subsequent section of AI in training will possibly be shaped through a balanced partnership among human educators and sensible systems—where AI supports, however does no longer update, the essential human elements of empathy, creativity, and ethical judgment in education.

As records indicates, AI's position in schooling isn't approximately changing teachers but empowering them—and helping each student realise their capability via shrewd, inclusive, and personalized mastering experiences.

CHAPTER 2

Personalized Education

2.1. AI and Student-Centered Education Models

Artificial intelligence (AI) has the potential to revolutionize the instructional landscape. In particular, student-centered education models have grow to be more green and effective with the help of AI technologies. Given that the fundamental purpose of schooling is to provide an revel in tailor-made to the desires, studying patterns, and interests of each pupil, the opportunities provided with the aid of AI are of superb importance.

Student-focused education offers an technique wherein every student gets an enjoy customized to their mastering pace, alternatives, and strengths. AI allows teachers to better understand their students and interfere in a manner that fits each student's getting to know technique. This is an educational philosophy that takes person variations inside the school room into consideration and facilitates every scholar reach their full capacity.

AI has the capability to locate college students' challenges for the duration of the mastering technique and offer suitable assist. For example, if a student is struggling with a specific subject matter, AI-powered structures can provide additional sources or advocate opportunity studying paths to cope with regions of misunderstanding more correctly. This process permits instructors to provide greater targeted and green remarks to students.

AI gives the ability to continuously display student overall performance. By analyzing college students' progress over the years, it is able to become aware of which areas they're excelling in and which regions require more interest. Such analyses offer instructors with the possibility to develop strategies tailor-made to every scholar's desires.

Students' progress may be tracked constantly with the aid of AI systems, allowing timely interventions while essential. This lets in teachers to approach every scholar in a way that aligns with their person requirements, making sure that the instructional system is as personalised as feasible for every learner.

Personalized training includes supplying materials and techniques which are customized consistent with college students' varying mastering styles and paces. AI can gather records on each scholar and create content material tailor-made to their character gaining knowledge of methods. This content material is formed based totally on the student's previous learning experiences, permitting the system to supply materials that are quality applicable to their modern desires.

Students can also have unique getting to know patterns, along with visible, auditory, or kinesthetic. AI can understand those one-of-a-kind gaining knowledge of patterns and select the most appropriate teaching strategies for every scholar. For instance, a student who learns excellent via visual way is probably supplied video-based content, whilst an auditory learner might be furnished with audio lectures or podcasts. Kinesthetic inexperienced persons, however, will be given more fingers-on sports or interactive materials.

Another vast gain of AI is its ability to offer instant feedback to college students. In traditional schooling, instructors take time to offer feedback while a scholar makes a mistake. However, AI structures can analyze a pupil's responses instantly and offer comments in real time. This hastens the learning manner and enables students apprehend their mistakes greater speedy.

AI-generated comments can also be personalized. It can offer precise pointers for improvement and provide approaches to accurate mistakes. Furthermore, AI permits students to song their own progress, as they are able to see what regions they've advanced in and what topics they still want to work on.

AI will play an increasingly more large role inside the destiny of pupil-targeted training models. As more customized and custom designed content material becomes available, AI technologies can be used greater successfully to manual every student via their own learning adventure. AI will now not simplest allow teachers to track their college students' development, however it's going to also help them broaden techniques to make their coaching techniques extra efficient.

AI-based totally training will make sure that the diverse mastering speeds inside the lecture room are addressed, creating an educational surroundings that is suited to every scholar. This is specially beneficial for college students who may additionally struggle or have gaps of their getting to know. Personalized studying, powered by using AI, will help students examine faster and offer them with a safer, greater effective mastering surroundings.

AI and student-targeted education models have the capacity to convert training structures. Tailored learning materials and actual-time comments could make gaining knowledge of strategies extra green. This approach creates a greater powerful academic environment not most effective for college kids but additionally for instructors. AI-supported training offers the possibility to track students' man or woman improvement and create customized strategies for every of them. In the future, broader integration of AI in schooling will represent a substantial step within the evolution of student-focused training fashions.

2.2. Personal Learning Plans and AI

Personalized gaining knowledge of plans are at the middle of present day educational practices that goal to cater to the individual desires and competencies of students. The integration of synthetic intelligence (AI) in those plans gives a transformative approach, taking into consideration a far more tailor-made and adaptive learning enjoy. By reading information from numerous resources, AI can assist educators create non-public mastering paths for college students, ensuring that every learner receives the guide and resources they need to be successful.

AI allows the advent of dynamic and individualized getting to know plans by means of assessing a scholar's previous knowledge, abilties, mastering options, and progress over time. These AI-powered mastering plans go past easy customization by using constantly adapting to the student's evolving desires, demanding situations, and successes. This customized approach contrasts with traditional one-length-suits-all coaching models, providing a more green and attractive manner for college students to analyze at their very own tempo.

AI systems utilize great amounts of facts to assemble personalised getting to know plans. By gathering statistics from pupil interactions, performance checks, and engagement with numerous studying substances, AI can build a complete profile of every scholar's strengths and weaknesses. This records-pushed approach allows AI to endorse unique sources, sporting activities, or activities so as to satisfactory address the pupil's desires.

For instance, a scholar suffering with a particular subject matter, which includes algebra, ought to have extra sports or explanatory videos suggested by way of an AI device. On the opposite hand, a student excelling in a subject can be supplied with more advanced content material to maintain them engaged and challenged. This degree of personalization ensures that scholars are continually running inside their sector of proximal development, a place where they're neither crushed nor beneath-challenged.

AI's capacity to technique information in actual time approach that mastering plans can be constantly up to date. As students whole assignments, tests, or learning activities, their performance is tracked and analyzed, permitting AI to alter the getting to know plan based totally on the brand new information. This makes mastering plans enormously dynamic and able to evolving alongside the student's boom.

One of the important thing blessings of AI is its role in adaptive learning technologies. These technology allow for the real-time change of the learning revel in based totally on student overall performance. For instance, AI can adapt the difficulty level of questions or duties in step with how properly a student is appearing. If a scholar is answering questions efficaciously effectively, the AI may gift greater difficult demanding situations to stimulate in addition increase. Conversely, if a student is struggling, the AI can offer less difficult duties or additional motives to assist them construct confidence and competence.

Adaptive mastering powered by AI ensures that each scholar is constantly engaged with content material this is at the correct degree of issue. This eliminates the frustrations of being too some distance ahead or too far in the back of the material and permits students to learn at their very own tempo with out feeling neglected or overwhelmed.

AI-pushed non-public getting to know plans empower students to take manipulate of their instructional adventure. As AI equipment provide customized hints and resources, students are given the autonomy to pick out how they have interaction with the content material. This level of personalization fosters a experience of possession over gaining knowledge of and encourages extra motivation and engagement. Students can explore regions of interest more deeply and development at their very own pace, even as receiving steering that is tailor-made mainly to their wishes.

AI-powered studying plans also can assist one-of-a-kind mastering patterns. Some college students might also benefit from video tutorials, whilst others might also study better via interactive sporting events or studying substances. AI systems can perceive those possibilities and offer tailor-made hints, ensuring that each scholar has get right of entry to to the only gaining knowledge of sources for their fashion.

Moreover, AI can offer immediately feedback to college students, letting them song their development and make adjustments to their gaining knowledge of technique if vital. This feedback loop encourages college students to take an lively position of their schooling, in addition growing their sense of company and self-direction.

A key function of AI-more suitable customized gaining knowledge of plans is the continuous tracking and adjustment of a student's learning direction. Unlike conventional strategies where a gaining knowledge of plan would possibly stay static for lengthy periods, AI structures can adapt the plan based on real-time statistics. For example, if a scholar starts to carry out better in a certain region, the AI gadget would possibly growth the complexity of obligations or introduce extra advanced content. Conversely, if the student struggles in a particular domain, the device can provide additional practice materials or trade reasons.

This potential to screen and adjust gaining knowledge of plans in actual time ensures that students are constantly receiving the proper stage of help. It also lets in educators to become aware of capacity areas of problem early, making it feasible to interfere before demanding situations become overwhelming for the scholar.

While AI can provide huge benefits in creating personalized getting to know paths, it's also vital for educators to be concerned inside the procedure. AI can provide effective insights and tips based on statistics, but it is ultimately as much as the instructor to apprehend the broader context of every scholar's needs, persona, and occasions. AI-supported gaining knowledge of plans must therefore be viewed as a tool that complements and enhances the educator's function as opposed to replaces it.

Teachers can use the insights supplied by using AI to make informed decisions approximately study room sports, group dynamics, and the allocation of resources. Additionally, instructors can collaborate with students and their families to ensure that studying plans are surely customized to fulfill each student's precise dreams and aspirations. This collaborative approach can help college students obtain their full ability and foster a greater supportive learning surroundings.

As AI era keeps to adapt, customized gaining knowledge of plans are anticipated to become even extra state-of-the-art. The integration of AI with rising technologies along with virtual and augmented truth, natural language processing, and gadget gaining knowledge of will further enhance the capacity to create completely personalised, immersive mastering studies. These advances will allow for even extra distinct and dynamic mastering paths, making education increasingly more customized to each man or woman's specific needs and possibilities.

The future of personalized learning plans powered by way of AI holds tremendous promise for education. As extra information becomes available and AI algorithms come to be greater delicate, students will advantage from even extra correct and powerful getting to know plans. This generation has the potential to offer a virtually individualized training experience, assisting college students attain their complete capacity in a manner that isn't feasible with traditional coaching methods.

Personal mastering plans powered via AI offer a transformative method to schooling. By making use of data-driven insights, AI can create particularly customized and dynamic learning pathways that meet the man or woman desires of students. With the capability to adapt in actual time, AI ensures that each scholar is supplied with the right stage of support and challenge, fostering extra engagement and achievement. As AI era maintains to improve, the capacity for further personalization and innovation in schooling is great, and it will certainly play a crucial function in shaping the destiny of mastering.

2.3. Data-Driven Educational Methods

Data-pushed academic techniques talk over with the use of facts and analytics to inform coaching practices, enhance getting to know consequences, and optimize instructional reviews. The growing availability of information in training—starting from pupil overall performance metrics to engagement stages and past—has revolutionized how educators method their teaching techniques. Artificial intelligence (AI) performs a pivotal position in harnessing this facts to power personalised, green, and effective mastering environments.

The use of facts in training isn't always a new concept. However, with improvements in generation and the proliferation of virtual gaining knowledge of equipment, the scope and intensity of instructional statistics have increased significantly. Data in education can come from various assets, consisting of standardized assessments, in-class tests, learning control structures (LMS), or even behavioral facts that tracks scholar engagement and interplay with studying substances.

At its center, information in training serves to offer a deeper information of student overall performance, mastering styles, and regions of improvement. When effectively gathered and analyzed, this records can offer insights into how college students analyze, what demanding situations they face, and which teaching techniques are best. Data-driven choice-making lets in educators to regulate their strategies in actual time and better address the numerous needs of students.

Artificial intelligence plays a massive position within the collection, evaluation, and interpretation of tutorial records. With its capability to method large amounts of facts fast and appropriately, AI can offer actionable insights that human educators might also forget about. AI-pushed systems can examine scholar responses, are expecting learning outcomes, and even identify capability gaining knowledge of gaps earlier than they emerge as extensive barriers.

For example, AI-powered studying management structures can song a scholar's development throughout more than one topics and provide unique reports on regions wherein the student is struggling. These insights may be used to layout targeted interventions and assets that assist students triumph over demanding situations and improve their understanding of the cloth.

AI also can manner behavioral information, together with how lengthy a scholar spends on a selected undertaking or how frequently they interact with learning assets. By reading this facts, AI can provide insights into the student's engagement degree, motivation, and emotional kingdom. This allows create a greater entire photo of the student's learning revel in, enabling educators to offer guide in which it is needed most.

Predictive analytics is every other key feature of information-driven instructional techniques, and AI enhances its ability appreciably. By studying historical information, AI systems can forecast destiny mastering results and pick out tendencies in pupil performance. Predictive models can help educators count on challenges inclusive of college students prone to falling at the back of, folks that may also want extra guide, or people who are possibly to excel and require more superior fabric.

For example, AI can expect which college students are liable to failing primarily based on their grades, attendance, and engagement with the course material. With this information, educators can interfere early to offer additional sources, tutoring, or personalized gaining knowledge of strategies. On the opposite hand, AI can also assist pick out students who're excelling and advocate enrichment opportunities to in addition venture them.

Predictive analytics also plays a important function in optimizing direction design. By reading information from beyond guides, educators can become aware of which content areas were most challenging for college kids, in which getting to know effects had been strongest, and wherein additional sources might be needed. This allows for the continuous improvement of curricula and ensures that coaching strategies are tailor-made to the needs of the cutting-edge cohort.

One of the most significant blessings of records-driven schooling is the capability to provide personalized learning studies. AI systems analyze records from a whole lot of assets to create individualized gaining knowledge of paths for college kids. These paths are dynamically adjusted based on actual-time information, making sure that each scholar receives the right amount of mission and help.

For instance, if a scholar demonstrates trouble with a particular subject matter, AI can recommend extra sources, alter the difficulty degree of tasks, or offer step-by way of-step factors to help the pupil better understand the fabric. On the other hand, if a pupil is progressing quick, AI can provide more superior content material to hold them engaged and challenged.

Data-driven interventions aren't handiest personalized but also particularly centered. Traditional instructional techniques regularly rely upon generalized methods that may not fully deal with the precise desires of every student. However, with the assist of AI and educational facts, interventions can be greater precise and aligned with the individual's studying profile. This outcomes in higher mastering results and a extra green use of instructional resources.

Data-driven methods also enable the supply of real-time remarks to students. Traditional instructional exams, consisting of end-of-time period tests or periodic assessments, offer a delayed photograph of pupil overall performance. In contrast, AI-pushed structures can offer immediate comments on pupil work, permitting beginners to recognize their mistakes and accurate them earlier than they accumulate.

For instance, AI structures in on line mastering systems can grade assignments right away and offer remarks on precise areas where the scholar went incorrect. This allows college students to check and refine their information proper away, promoting a greater green and tasty learning technique. Real-time feedback fosters a growth attitude by way of reinforcing the concept that mistakes are part of the studying manner, main to continuous improvement.

Additionally, the actual-time nature of statistics collection and analysis lets in educators to regulate their teaching techniques on the fly. If a selected lesson or interest isn't resonating with college students, educators can without delay alter their method based totally on the records insights provided with the aid of AI structures. This flexibility and adaptableness are key to fostering an environment in which college students can thrive.

While AI structures and facts-driven methods mostly focus on student results, they also offer extensive advantages to instructors. By reading instructional records, AI can help educators become greater effective in their coaching methods. AI-powered tools can identify which coaching strategies are most a success with precise groups of college students, which gaining knowledge of sports cause the finest engagement, and which regions require additional interest.

For example, AI can analyze how different coaching methods have an effect on student studying consequences. If a certain approach works nicely for visible newbies however not for auditory rookies, the information can assist teachers modify their educational techniques to better meet the needs of diverse rookies. This lets in for the non-stop development of coaching practices and ensures that educators are the use of proof-based totally methods that align with pupil wishes.

Moreover, AI-driven analytics can help reduce teacher workload via automating responsibilities inclusive of grading and administrative obligations. This offers educators more time to focus on direct student interplay and personalized coaching. By freeing up time, information-driven methods allow instructors to concentrate on what subjects most—enticing with students and fostering a superb learning surroundings.

As technology continues to increase, the capability for statistics-pushed academic techniques will only increase. The integration of AI with rising technologies which includes gadget gaining knowledge of, herbal language processing, and cognitive computing will enable even deeper insights into scholar learning styles and behaviors. These developments promise to create even extra customized, powerful, and inclusive learning reviews.

Furthermore, the developing use of information in education raises important questions about facts privacy and safety. As educational data will become more special and granular, it is important to ensure that sensitive student records is protected and used ethically. Proper statistics governance frameworks could be necessary to guard privacy at the same time as still permitting the blessings of data-driven schooling.

Data-driven educational techniques powered by using AI are transforming the manner educators educate and students examine. Through the evaluation of significant amounts of tutorial statistics, AI is permitting personalised gaining knowledge of stories, predictive analytics, and actual-time feedback, all of which make contributions to better getting to know outcomes. As AI continues to adapt, the capability for more focused and powerful interventions will make bigger, making education more tailor-made and attentive to person wishes. With cautious attention to statistics privacy and moral concerns, information-pushed methods will maintain to form the future of education in profound methods.

2.4. Gamification and AI in Learning Paths

The integration of gamification with synthetic intelligence in instructional environments represents a transformative evolution in how mastering is designed, introduced, and skilled. As conventional models of guidance conflict to maintain engagement inside the digital age, educators and developers have became toward sport-primarily based mechanics to reignite student motivation. Simultaneously, AI technology have enabled exceptional stages of adaptability and personalization, allowing these gamified stories to be tailor-made to man or woman newcomers in real-time. The convergence of those two effective paradigms—gamification and AI—has no longer most effective redefined the structure of gaining knowledge of paths however also increased the function of learners from passive recipients to lively members in their educational journeys.

Gamification, in its essence, involves the application of sport design factors including factors, tiers, demanding situations, badges, leaderboards, and rewards into non-game contexts, mainly training. The psychological underpinnings of gamification are rooted in motivation theories, mainly self-dedication idea, which emphasizes the want for autonomy, competence, and relatedness. In studying environments, these needs translate into interactive and rewarding experiences that foster deeper cognitive engagement. However, on its own, gamification can fall into the trap of being one-size-fits-all—motivating for some students but useless or even frustrating for others. This is wherein AI intervenes as a crucial companion, enabling gamified systems to be not most effective engaging however also dynamically adaptive.

AI algorithms in current studying systems can analyze large amounts of learner information—starting from behavioral metrics like time-on-undertaking, blunders styles, and interplay sequences, to cognitive indicators along with problem degree mastery and engagement drop-off factors. Using this records, AI can form the gamified shape of a route to align with a learner's person alternatives, goals, and performance traits. For example, a pupil who continuously responds nicely to task-primarily based obligations might be offered with an increasing number of complicated sport-like missions, at the same time as any other who well-knownshows anxiety under aggressive stress might be presented a extra exploratory and narrative-pushed getting to know direction.

One of the most huge contributions of AI in gamified gaining knowledge of is real-time comments. Unlike traditional structures that offer standardized or not on time remarks, AI-enabled platforms can interpret a learner's development within the moment and provide tailored guidance, encouragement, or corrective support. For example, intelligent tutoring systems embedded inside a gamified surroundings can simulate an interactive sport master that adjusts the narrative or degree development based totally on how well the learner is internalizing standards. This guarantees that novices stay inside their most beneficial region of improvement, warding off each boredom from tasks that are too easy and frustration from demanding situations which are too difficult.

Another key detail of this synergy is the dynamic technology of content. Through herbal language processing and procedural content generation, AI can create new scenarios, questions, or challenges within a gamified system, making the studying enjoy sense clean and less repetitive. Language mastering apps like Duolingo, as an example, use AI to determine the perfect stability of review versus new content, adjusting lesson formats and problem degrees in line with the person's performance and ancient mastering curve. The gamified rewards—streaks, hearts, crowns—are not applied uniformly but are algorithmically tuned to boost the right learning behaviors for every individual.

Gamification additionally thrives on storytelling, and AI plays a crucial role in personalizing narratives that unfold as novices progress via academic responsibilities. Through sentiment evaluation and studying analytics, AI can verify emotional engagement and adjust tale arcs or person interactions to better resonate with the learner. In immersive environments, such as digital fact lecture rooms or AI-driven academic video games, this capability turns abstract concepts into lived experiences. For instance, a student gaining knowledge of environmental technology may embark on an AI-personalized sport adventure in which their in-game selections—subsidized by way of real science content material—have an effect on ecosystems, triggering precise storylines and outcomes that deepen understanding.

The motivational electricity of opposition and collaboration—center factors in gamification—is likewise more advantageous through AI. Leaderboards, traditionally static and often demotivating to lower-ranked students, can now be dynamically segmented with the aid of AI into extra psychologically secure groupings, making sure that each one learners enjoy workable fulfillment. AI can create "shadow competitors," bots that simulate peers at similar talent levels, permitting inexperienced persons to experience a feel of progression and mastery with out the bad social contrast consequences frequently discovered in real-international leaderboards.

Furthermore, AI helps the layout of getting to know quests and adaptive missions. These are established pathways composed of small, game-like demanding situations that cumulatively educate a concept or talent. Rather than predefining a static collection of responsibilities, AI observes how a learner performs and reorders, modifies, or maybe omits positive elements to maximize effectiveness. A struggling scholar would possibly acquire more foundational quests with better on the spot praise values, even as an advanced learner would possibly face complicated puzzles and receive symbolic rather than extrinsic rewards. Over time, the AI fashions evolve with the learner, exceptional-tuning the gamified environment for most excellent cognitive stimulation and emotional pride.

Importantly, the convergence of gamification and AI additionally introduces new possibilities for assessment. Traditional checks frequently disrupt the flow of gaining knowledge of and might fail to capture nuanced skills. In comparison, AI-driven gamified environments allow for stealth assessment—a technique wherein freshmen are evaluated constantly via their gameplay movements without being openly tested. These exams are embedded within the getting to know experience, and AI makes use of them to update learner profiles in actual time. This allows educators to get hold of granular insights into learner increase, misconceptions, and learning alternatives with out interrupting the engagement.

Despite its transformative potential, the combination of AI and gamification in education is not with out challenges. The moral implications of behavior manipulation, records privacy, and motivational dependence on outside rewards require careful attention. Over-reliance on gamified AI structures could lessen intrinsic motivation or commodify gaining knowledge of into a set of responsibilities and rewards. Additionally, bias in AI algorithms or a bad information of pupil psychology in game layout may want to lead to exclusion or disengagement amongst certain learner populations. Ensuring that AI-superior gamified systems are obvious, inclusive, and aligned with pedagogical dreams is vital.

Educators have to additionally be empowered to understand and utilize those gear correctly. Professional development applications need to consist of education within the ideas of gamification, the fundamentals of AI literacy, and ethical technology use. Only then can educators meaningfully combine these systems into curricula in place of the usage of them as superficial add-ons.

Looking forward, the fusion of AI and gamification guarantees a fair more immersive and responsive academic landscape. Emerging technologies like emotion popularity, mind-laptop interfaces, and augmented reality will in addition decorate the depth and interactivity of learning video games. AI could be able to apprehend symptoms of fatigue, frustration, or confusion and modify the game dynamics therefore—possibly pausing the mission, transferring to a exclusive modality, or injecting humor or empathy thru virtual avatars.

In addition, the increasing sophistication of AI fashions will allow for hyper-customized gamified gaining knowledge of environments in which each scholar basically plays a uniquely tailored sport, grounded in rigorous pedagogy but fashioned via their very own curiosity, habits, and pace. These getting to know environments may go beyond conventional subjects, mixing interdisciplinary content with actual-international hassle solving in methods that are each significant and motivating.

The transformation of gaining knowledge of paths through the integration of gamification and AI isn't always merely a technological improve; it represents a fundamental rethinking of the instructional method. It positions novices as heroes in their personal instructional narratives, supported with the aid of shrewd systems that adapt, guide, and encourage. In doing so, it lays the basis for a future wherein schooling isn't only greater powerful however also more completely satisfied, inclusive, and human-focused—even when introduced thru machines.

Gamification and AI, whilst harmonized thoughtfully, offer an great promise: learning that seems like play however achieves the intensity of scholarship; structures that understand college students now not as data points, but as evolving minds; and school rooms which are as dynamic and attractive as the sector students are being organized to trade.

2.5. AI-Driven Mentoring and Tutoring Systems

Artificial Intelligence (AI) has an increasing number of end up a transformative pressure in schooling, no longer simply as a device for content transport however as an smart facilitator of customized steering, mentoring, and tutoring. Traditional instructional models often fall quick in addressing the numerous learning wishes of college students, in particular in huge or resource-limited settings. In assessment, AI-pushed mentoring and tutoring structures offer scalable, adaptive, and constantly available help, reshaping the position of practise through mimicking and augmenting human steering. These systems constitute a paradigm shift in how mentorship and academic assistance are conceptualized and brought—making getting to know more available, responsive, and personally tailored.

At their center, AI-pushed mentoring and tutoring systems aim to copy or decorate the aid that a human teach or mentor offers. This includes clarifying complex standards, guiding trouble-solving techniques, offering emotional encouragement, and adapting instructional strategies to in shape man or woman learner profiles. With improvements in machine studying, natural language processing (NLP), know-how illustration, and person modeling, these systems have advanced a long way past their early prototypes. Today, they are able to simulate talk, examine learning conduct in real-time, customize instructional pathways, and even reply empathetically to learner feelings.

One of the earliest applications of AI in tutoring turned into the improvement of Intelligent Tutoring Systems (ITS) within the 1980s and 1990s. These structures, along with Carnegie Mellon University's Cognitive Tutor and the University of Memphis' AutoTutor, have been constructed upon rule-based AI that encoded domain know-how and pedagogical understanding. They employed a 3-tier structure: a site model representing the problem count number, a student model tracking the learner's knowledge and progress, and a pedagogical version figuring out academic techniques. Although those systems had been groundbreaking, they had been frequently inflexible, expensive to construct, and confined to unique issue regions like algebra or physics.

With the upward push of big facts, cloud computing, and advanced machine learning strategies within the 2010s, AI-pushed tutoring systems underwent a primary transformation. Modern structures are not restrained to predefined policies and decision trees; alternatively, they leverage predictive analytics and sample reputation to conform dynamically. Systems like Knewton, ALEKS, and Squirrel AI in China use large datasets to pick out mastering gaps, expect outcomes, and modify content shipping in actual time. These platforms continuously analyze from consumer interactions, refining their academic techniques to better in shape the learner's cognitive kingdom, pace, and preferences.

A defining characteristic of AI-driven tutoring systems nowadays is their ability for non-stop and formative assessment. Unlike conventional checks that provide remarks after the truth, AI tutors can reveal every keystroke, answer, hesitation, and click on—growing a wealthy behavioral profile of the scholar. From this information, the system can infer no longer handiest mastery of content material however additionally gaining knowledge of strategies, motivation tiers, or even emotional states. For instance, if a pupil is again and again making careless errors or showing signs and symptoms of disengagement, the AI might intervene with encouraging messages, offer a evaluate module, or shift to a one of a kind educational format.

Natural language processing has additionally revolutionized AI-driven mentoring by using allowing systems to apprehend and generate human-like dialogue. Virtual sellers, such as chatbots or voice-based totally tutors, can now behavior contextual conversations, provide an explanation for ideas, ask probing questions, and provide personalised recommendation. These retailers are able to simulating Socratic thinking strategies, encouraging students to assume critically and articulate their reasoning. Some platforms integrate speech recognition and sentiment analysis to come across tone, strain, and affective cues, allowing the gadget to respond empathetically and adjust its demeanor.

Beyond challenge-precise tutoring, AI is now getting into the world of holistic mentoring—imparting steering on intention setting, time control, have a look at habits, and even profession improvement. Virtual mentors like IBM's Watson Tutor or AI partners in education platforms can help students in mapping out instructional plans, suggesting courses aligned with career interests, and presenting reminders and motivational nudges. These systems draw on significant knowledge graphs, consumer histories, and predictive fashions to make clever hints that evolve because the scholar progresses.

AI mentoring is specially treasured in contexts in which human mentoring sources are scarce or erratically to be had. In underfunded faculties, faraway regions, or at some point of worldwide disruptions just like the COVID-19 pandemic, AI systems have provided continuity and fairness in instructional support. They provide 24/7 accessibility, multilingual competencies, and the potential to serve thousands of students simultaneously without degrading the great of guidance. This scalability makes AI-driven mentoring a promising solution for addressing educational disparities and democratizing access to satisfactory mastering support.

Another emerging fashion is the mixing of AI-pushed tutoring into collaborative and social mastering environments. Platforms are now exploring how AI can facilitate peer tutoring, organization take a look at periods, and discussion forums. For instance, AI can examine a collection's communique to pick out misconceptions, spotlight treasured contributions, or suggest assets. It can also fit college students with complementary strengths and weaknesses for peer mentoring. In doing so, AI now not best helps character freshmen however additionally enhances the dynamics of collaborative learning.

Despite these advantages, the implementation of AI-driven mentoring and tutoring structures comes with essential challenges. A primary subject is the ethical use of pupil facts. These systems require get admission to to distinctive non-public information, including academic facts, behavioral patterns, and sometimes even biometric records. Ensuring that records is accrued transparently, stored securely, and used responsibly is critical. There is likewise the chance of algorithmic bias—wherein AI structures may also unintentionally enhance existing inequities or provide irrelevant guidelines based on wrong training facts.

The emotional and relational size of human mentoring is every other area in which AI nonetheless faces obstacles. While

AI tutors can simulate empathy to some extent, they lack actual understanding, cultural nuance, and the moral compass that human mentors carry. Over-reliance on AI structures may want to inadvertently devalue the human components of education that foster identity, resilience, and ethical thinking. As such, AI-pushed mentoring ought to be visible as a complement, not a replacement, to human help.

To cope with these issues, hybrid fashions of mentoring and tutoring are gaining reputation. In such fashions, AI provides baseline help—handling recurring queries, offering content material hints, and monitoring progress—even as human educators step in for complicated, emotional, or moral troubles. Teachers can use AI-generated dashboards to reveal pupil progress, perceive at-risk novices, and tailor their interventions greater efficiently. This partnership between human and device enhances each scalability and pleasant.

From a design perspective, the achievement of AI mentoring structures depends on their usability, transparency, and alignment with pedagogical goals. Interfaces have to be intuitive, culturally sensitive, and attractive. The logic behind AI pointers need to be explainable to each college students and educators, fostering consider and expertise. Furthermore, these systems must be evaluated continuously to make sure they may be assembly gaining knowledge of goals and adapting to numerous student wishes.

Looking beforehand, the destiny of AI-driven mentoring and tutoring is possibly to be formed by several technological and societal tendencies. The creation of massive language models, which includes GPT-based structures, is enabling extra fluent, contextual, and multi-flip dialogues that closely resemble human verbal exchange. AI becomes more proactive, expecting learner wishes and beginning interventions earlier than troubles rise up. Advances in affective computing will permit structures to reply more sensitively to pupil emotions, reducing tension and improving engagement.

Moreover, the convergence of AI with virtual reality (VR) and augmented reality (AR) will create immersive tutoring reviews. Learners would possibly enter digital labs, historical simulations, or collaborative hassle-fixing arenas wherein AI mentors manual them thru complex obligations in rich, interactive environments. These reports will now not handiest decorate mastering results but additionally prepare college students for future offices that call for adaptability, creativity, and technological fluency.

AI-pushed mentoring and tutoring structures are not just a technological innovation; they constitute a reimagination of the educational system. By supplying personalised, well timed, and scalable guide, they've the capability to shut achievement gaps, foster lifelong learning, and empower college students to take ownership of their instructional trips. However, figuring out this capability requires considerate layout, ethical governance, and a clean knowledge of the complementary roles that people and machines play within the learning technique.

In a world wherein know-how is increasing swiftly and traditional instructional models are increasingly more strained, AI-pushed mentors and tutors provide a vision of getting to know this is responsive, inclusive, and future-prepared. Their achievement will rely now not on how well they mimic humans, however on how accurately we use them to aid the human spirit of interest, boom, and connection.

2.6. Adapting Content Delivery with AI

The process of content shipping in training has historically accompanied a uniform, linear, and standardized method. Whether in physical classrooms, textbooks, or early e-studying environments, students have long been subjected to the same tempo, the identical substances, and the equal academic strategies—regardless of their personal learning needs, abilties, or hobbies. This version, even though green for mass schooling, fails to account for the big heterogeneity amongst learners. With the emergence and maturation of synthetic intelligence (AI), this long-status tension is present process a fundamental transformation. AI is not merely supplementing content delivery—it's far revolutionizing it via adapting materials dynamically, tailoring the educational adventure to every learner in actual time, and creating an environment in which education responds to the man or woman, as opposed to the person conforming to the machine.

Adapting content delivery with AI refers back to the system through which smart structures regulate the layout, shape, timing, issue, modality, or even the collection of learning materials based on the continuously monitored overall performance, choices, and wishes of every scholar. Unlike static systems, AI-enabled structures use facts-driven insights to make pedagogical choices formerly reserved for expert human instructors. The result is a greater personalised, enticing, and powerful learning enjoy.

At the heart of this edition process is the ability of AI to acquire, interpret, and act upon tremendous arrays of learner facts. This includes not most effective quantitative records consisting of take a look at rankings, time spent on duties, click on patterns, and answer accuracy, but additionally extra nuanced signs like hesitation costs, reaction self belief, facial expressions (in video-primarily based structures), voice tone, and sentiment evaluation. By aggregating this statistics and feeding it into predictive models and studying algorithms, AI systems increase complete learner profiles that inform how, while, and what content material should be delivered.

One of the earliest manifestations of AI-tailored content material delivery is seen in adaptive mastering structures including DreamBox (for arithmetic), Smart Sparrow (for higher training), and Knewton (for various K-12 subjects).

These structures constantly determine freshmen' responses to instructional content and use algorithms to determine the following appropriate activity. For example, if a pupil constantly struggles with multi-digit multiplication however excels in conceptual word problems, the system can adapt via providing greater visible aids, breaking down the content into smaller steps, and reinforcing foundational arithmetic skills before reintroducing complexity.

AI not most effective adapts the issue level however also the modality of content. Some rookies may additionally thrive while presented with visible explanations, at the same time as others can also require auditory narratives or palms-on simulations. AI structures, prepared with machine learning abilties, can come across which codecs produce the very best engagement and retention for every learner and ultimately gift substances in the handiest shape. A student studying cell biology, for instance, might be given an interactive 3D model of a cellular, while some other can also receive a narrated animation or a textual content-based educational, relying on their past interactions and performance metrics.

Moreover, herbal language processing (NLP) has dramatically elevated AI's potential to deliver custom designed content material in linguistic shape. AI-driven structures can now generate reasons, paraphrase complex thoughts, and respond to scholar queries the use of conversational language that aligns with the learner's analyzing level and vocabulary utilization. Chatbots and digital tutors powered through big language fashions are more and more able to retaining significant, context-conscious dialogues, supplying definitions, clarifications, and examples tailor-made to a learner's contemporary stage of knowledge.

In language studying applications, along with Duolingo or Elsa Speak, AI not best adapts the content however also the pacing, accessory, feedback kind, or even the frequency of review. These systems examine pronunciation, grammar mistakes, and person engagement to deliver exercise physical activities that fill information gaps with out overwhelming the learner. The intention is to hold an most useful balance among mission and support—a balance that academic theorists consult with as the "zone of proximal improvement." AI structures dynamically searching for this region for each pupil, making sure the content material is neither too clean nor too tough.

Another important area of AI-tailored content material shipping is in assessment-driven gaining knowledge of. Here, formative tests are embedded seamlessly into the learning revel in, and their results at once have an effect on the subsequent content added. Instead of looking ahead to give up-of-unit exams, AI systems compare learning continuously. Based on performance in micro-checks, the AI decides whether to enhance the pupil, revisit positive topics, or gift content thru alternative examples and analogies. This creates a remarks loop wherein evaluation and guidance are intertwined, enhancing each efficacy and efficiency.

AI also performs a widespread function in adapting content sequencing—figuring out the order wherein subjects or talents are delivered. While conventional curricula observe a linear development, AI permits for nonlinear, bendy pathways that adapt based on learner progression. For example, in a pc science route, a student would possibly skip fundamental conditional common sense if their overall performance suggests mastery, and as an alternative be directed to extra superior algorithmic questioning duties. Conversely, another learner suffering with syntax is probably supplied with extra foundational modules before intending. This lets in for differentiated education at scale.

Beyond person edition, AI is increasingly more used to tailor content material delivery at the school room or cohort level. Intelligent structures can examine aggregated data from an entire magnificence and recommend differentiated lesson plans for the trainer, grouping college students by way of getting to know desires, styles, or progress. This allows extra powerful classroom management and guarantees that each one college students receive appropriate educational guide, even in various or mixed-ability classrooms.

Contextual model is every other rising frontier. AI structures are beginning to recall the learner's environment, emotional kingdom, and cognitive load. If a scholar is the usage of a cellular device in a noisy or distracting environment, the gadget may additionally shift to shorter, extra focused obligations. If the pupil appears fatigued or emotionally disengaged (detected thru webcam-based totally emotion recognition or behavioral evaluation), the system may pause the lesson, offer a motivational video, or switch to a game-based totally interest to restore cognizance. These context-aware variations beautify not handiest mastering outcomes however additionally well-being and motivation.

Furthermore, AI can support multilingual content material shipping and actual-time translation, making education more inclusive for linguistically diverse populations. A single lesson can be mechanically rendered in more than one languages, or speech recognition can help students in practising pronunciation with on the spot corrective comments. AI also can adapt cultural references and examples in content material to align with a learner's heritage, improving relatability and comprehension.

As adaptive content shipping turns into greater state-of-the-art, ethical considerations turn out to be paramount. Personalizing content material entails accumulating and analyzing sensitive student facts. Ensuring transparency in how information is used, preserving robust safety protocols, and giving students and educators control over personalization settings are vital for maintaining trust and protecting privacy.

Moreover, care should be taken to make sure that model does no longer inadvertently toughen stereotypes or restrict exposure to diverse content. For instance, if an AI system always assigns less difficult substances to students who first of all struggle, it can cap their potential instead of project them to develop.

Another task lies in making sure pedagogical coherence. While AI can optimize content shipping for individual customers, it should accomplish that within a curriculum that maintains conceptual integrity and aligns with studying requirements. The aim isn't to deliver random fragments of studying but to manual newcomers via coherent, significant, and cumulative reports. This requires careful collaboration between AI developers, educators, and academic designers.

Looking forward, the position of AI in adapting content shipping is likely to deepen. Advances in generative AI will allow structures to create entirely new content at the fly— generating examples, quizzes, simulations, or studying passages tailor-made to person gaining knowledge of desires and contexts. Integration with augmented truth (AR) and digital truth (VR) will offer immersive, adaptive content material that reacts to inexperienced persons' movements, choices, and overall performance in actual-time. Emotionally smart AI will similarly refine how content material is added, responding not most effective to cognitive indicators however additionally to affective states.

AI will also play a vital position in lifelong learning, helping adults reskill and upskill correctly. Personalized getting to know pathways could be dynamically generated primarily based on career dreams, existing abilities, and studying history, guiding learners via adaptive micro-credentials and modular training ecosystems.

Adapting content shipping with AI marks a profound shift in academic philosophy and exercise. It transforms education from a static, mass-produced carrier right into a dynamic, learner-focused enjoy. By continuously reading, adjusting, and optimizing how content is brought, AI permits deeper information, sustained engagement, and equitable get entry to to first-rate training. While challenges continue to be, the capacity to tailor education to the unique rhythm, fashion, and potential of every learner is not dream—it's miles an unfolding fact.

CHAPTER 3

Artificial Intelligence Assisted Classrooms

3.1. AI's Physical and Digital Role in Education

The integration of artificial intelligence into education has caused a profound transformation in both the physical and virtual dimensions of learning environments. AI's presence in lecture rooms extends beyond software programs to consist of robot assistants, adaptive mastering platforms, and smart infrastructure that complements the performance of teaching and studying. In the digital realm, AI-pushed systems facilitate customized studying, automate administrative responsibilities, and offer real-time comments to college students and educators. Understanding the multifaceted function of AI in schooling requires analyzing its impact on conventional school rooms, on line getting to know structures, and the evolving courting between generation and pedagogy.

One of the maximum visible components of AI in training is its presence in bodily classrooms. Schools worldwide are adopting smart boards, AI-pushed tutoring robots, and voice assistants to beautify interactive getting to know. These equipment serve as supplementary educators, helping teachers in handing over instructions, answering pupil inquiries, and presenting individualized gaining knowledge of pathways.

Robotic teaching assistants, as an instance, had been delivered in numerous educational settings to guide college students in subjects like mathematics, technology, and language studying. These AI-powered assistants can recognize scholar feelings, respond to questions, and adapt their teaching techniques based totally on character mastering styles. Their capability to method and analyze student responses in real-time lets in for dynamic lesson adjustments, ensuring that students receive tailored guidance applicable to their needs.

Another massive software of AI in bodily lecture rooms is using clever surveillance and lecture room management structures. AI-powered cameras can music scholar engagement, locate symptoms of distraction, and even assess participation levels. This statistics helps teachers refine their teaching techniques and foster a extra enticing lecture room environment. Additionally, AI can automate administrative obligations along with attendance tracking, grading assignments, and organizing lesson plans, thereby decreasing the workload of educators.

Beyond the bodily lecture room, AI plays a important function in shaping virtual schooling. Online studying structures leverage AI to deliver personalised content, determine scholar development, and endorse sources based on character performance. AI-powered mastering management systems (LMS) can track student conduct, identify gaining knowledge of gaps, and advise tailored physical activities to enhance comprehension.

One of the most transformative aspects of AI in digital education is adaptive mastering. Unlike conventional one-length-fits-all teaching techniques, adaptive learning systems use AI algorithms to research pupil responses and alter the problem stage of sporting activities in actual time. These structures help students development at their own tempo, reinforcing principles they warfare with while skipping over fabric they have got already mastered. This technique notably complements learning efficiency and retention.

AI-powered chatbots and digital tutors have additionally turn out to be critical additives of virtual getting to know environments. These gear provide instantaneous assistance to students, answering queries and guiding them thru complex concepts. In higher education, AI-pushed research assistants help college students analyze substantial quantities of records, summarize educational papers, or even generate insights primarily based on machine gaining knowledge of models.

As schooling evolves right into a hybrid model that mixes in-individual and online coaching, AI bridges the distance between physical and virtual mastering. AI-powered collaboration equipment allow seamless communication between students and teachers, regardless of their place. Features like automatic transcription, actual-time translation, and AI-generated summaries help make instructional content extra accessible to diverse newbies.

AI also performs a crucial function in assessing student overall performance in hybrid studying environments. Traditional tests are being supplemented or replaced with the aid of AI-pushed assessments that examine a pupil's understanding through continuous evaluation rather than unmarried take a look at scores. AI systems can stumble on patterns in pupil conduct, predict educational results, and offer intervention techniques to prevent learning setbacks.

Despite its severa blessings, the implementation of AI in schooling increases ethical and logistical challenges. The reliance on AI-powered surveillance gear, as an instance, sparks concerns about pupil privateness and facts security. Schools and establishments must ensure that AI systems observe ethical guidelines to prevent biases, statistics breaches, and misuse of scholar information.

Moreover, there may be an ongoing debate approximately the role of AI in changing human educators. While AI can decorate getting to know studies, it can't reflect the human touch, emotional intelligence, and mentorship supplied through instructors. Instead of changing educators, AI need to be viewed as a tool that augments their abilities, allowing them to attention on crucial thinking, creativity, and interpersonal abilties.

AI's position in schooling spans both bodily and digital realms, revolutionizing how students learn and instructors coach. From AI-powered robots in school rooms to adaptive mastering systems in on-line training, AI-pushed innovations retain to reshape the getting to know landscape. However, the achievement of AI integration depends on ethical considerations, effective implementation, and a balanced method that continues the important human factors of schooling. As AI technology continues to conform, its effect on education will absolutely grow, supplying new opportunities to decorate accessibility, engagement, and customized getting to know experiences.

3.2. Teacher-Student Interaction in AI-Enhanced Education

Artificial intelligence is revolutionizing the manner teachers and college students interact in academic settings. Traditional coaching techniques depend upon direct communique, face-to-face engagement, and based curricula. However, AI-pushed equipment are reshaping those dynamics via introducing customized gaining knowledge of experiences, automated remarks mechanisms, and clever tutoring systems. While AI can facilitate greater efficient studying, the essential question remains: How does AI effect instructor-pupil relationships? This section explores the evolving role of AI inside the lecture room, its impact on trainer-pupil interactions, and the demanding situations of integrating AI whilst keeping the human essence of schooling.

AI serves as a bridge between students and instructors through automating administrative responsibilities, supplying customized pointers, and enhancing engagement. AI-powered platforms analyze pupil performance in real time, permitting teachers to cognizance on individualized guidance as opposed to spending excessive time on grading, lesson making plans, and evaluation.

For instance, AI-driven mastering control structures (LMS) music college students' progress and offer personalized content. These systems discover regions where college students war and advocate tailor-made physical games, enabling instructors to provide focused assist. AI additionally assists in language translation, making training greater reachable in multilingual lecture rooms.

Additionally, chatbots and virtual assistants permit students to invite questions each time, even out of doors school hours. AI tutors offer on the spot remarks, allowing students to exercise concepts at their very own pace. This reduces the burden on teachers at the same time as ensuring that students get hold of continuous support.

However, while AI improves performance, it does now not update the human connection between teachers and college students. Emotional guide, mentorship, and motivation remain vital elements of education that AI can not absolutely mirror.

One of AI's maximum massive contributions to training is personalised gaining knowledge of. Unlike conventional strategies that deal with all college students the equal, AI adapts preparation to person learning styles, preferences, and development.

AI-powered adaptive getting to know systems examine pupil facts and modify lesson problem thus. For instance, if a student struggles with algebra, the gadget affords extra physical activities, step-by-step factors, and alternative problem-solving processes. Conversely, if a scholar excels, AI introduces extra advanced principles, preserving them engaged.

From a trainer's angle, personalized gaining knowledge of enables them identify struggling students and intervene before overall performance declines. Teachers can use AI-generated reports to song student engagement, participation, and comprehension, letting them tailor their teaching techniques.

However, customized learning also gives demanding situations. Over-reliance on AI-pushed systems may lessen face-to-face interplay among teachers and students. If students on the whole interact with AI rather than their teachers, they will miss opportunities to broaden critical thinking, collaboration, and social capabilities. Striking a balance among AI-pushed personalization and direct human interplay is essential.

AI complements pupil engagement by way of creating interactive mastering reviews. Gamification, virtual reality (VR), and AI-generated simulations make training more immersive and enjoyable. For example, AI-driven language learning apps use speech reputation and adaptive quizzes to improve fluency. Similarly, VR-powered AI packages permit students to discover ancient activities, conduct virtual technological know-how experiments, and engage with complicated concepts in a arms-on manner.

AI additionally performs a position in fostering collaboration. Intelligent dialogue forums analyze pupil contributions and propose applicable subjects, encouraging deeper discussions. AI-powered peer evaluation equipment facilitate optimistic feedback, allowing students to research from each other.

Despite these advancements, AI-driven engagement should complement in place of replace human interplay. The role of a trainer extends past handing over content; they inspire interest, inspire creativity, and offer emotional help. While AI enhances participation, the trainer stays the cornerstone of a meaningful academic enjoy.

Integrating AI into teacher-student interactions provides numerous demanding situations:

1. Over-Reliance on AI – If AI handles most student interactions, the teacher's function may additionally end up secondary. Students might also end up depending on AI for answers in place of developing hassle-solving abilties.

2. Privacy and Data Security – AI systems acquire full-size amounts of student records. Ensuring that this statistics is blanketed and used ethically is crucial to keeping consider.

3. Equity and Accessibility – AI-driven education ought to be inclusive. Disparities in get entry to to AI tools should widen the virtual divide, disadvantaging students in underprivileged areas.

4. Bias in AI Algorithms – AI systems ought to study on various datasets to avoid biases that may have an effect on personalised studying guidelines.

5. Human Connection in Learning – Education is not pretty much understanding transfer; it's miles approximately mentorship, encouragement, and human connection. AI need to help in place of replace human relationships in the classroom.

AI is reworking trainer-scholar interactions through personalizing mastering, automating responsibilities, and improving engagement. While AI improves performance, it can't replace the mentorship, emotional help, and creativity that instructors deliver to the school room. The challenge is to integrate AI in a manner that enhances instead of diminishes human interplay. By striking this stability, AI can emerge as a effective ally in education, empowering both teachers and students inside the getting to know manner.

3.3. Smart Classrooms and Educational Technology

The concept of smart classrooms has revolutionized conventional schooling by using integrating artificial intelligence (AI), machine studying, and advanced virtual technologies into the mastering environment. As AI-pushed academic equipment turn out to be extra sophisticated, they're reshaping how teachers teach and how students learn. Smart classrooms provide customized studying, interactive reports, and automatic assessment techniques that beautify academic consequences. However, integrating those technology also provides demanding situations related to accessibility, privateness, and the evolving position of educators. This segment explores the effect of smart school rooms, the position of AI-pushed academic generation, and the future of virtual learning environments.

Smart classrooms have advanced substantially from conventional coaching strategies that trusted textbooks, chalkboards, and direct trainer-led education. The integration of virtual tools began with projectors, online sources, and early mastering management systems (LMS). Today, AI-powered clever school rooms use real-time records evaluation, adaptive getting to know systems, and interactive technology to create dynamic mastering environments.

Key features of smart lecture rooms consist of:

- AI-pushed adaptive gaining knowledge of that personalizes instruction based totally on man or woman pupil performance.

- Augmented truth (AR) and virtual reality (VR) for immersive mastering studies.

- Interactive whiteboards and virtual collaboration gear that beautify engagement.

- Automated attendance and assessment structures powered through AI analytics.

- AI chatbots and virtual assistants that provide real-time aid for students and instructors.

These technologies permit educators to move past one-size-fits-all coaching strategies, making sure that each student receives personalised practise suitable to their mastering tempo and fashion.

AI-driven instructional generation is fundamentally remodeling how educators train via automating routine tasks, enhancing curriculum layout, and presenting data-pushed insights.

AI reduces the administrative workload for teachers, permitting them to awareness on direct scholar engagement. Tasks along with grading assignments, scheduling, and attendance monitoring are more and more managed via AI-powered systems.

For example, AI-assisted grading tools analyze pupil responses and offer immediate feedback, saving educators hours of guide grading. Automated attendance systems use facial popularity to track student presence, putting off the need for guide roll calls.

One of the most substantial advantages of AI in smart lecture rooms is its capacity to tailor lessons to individual students. Adaptive gaining knowledge of structures analyze overall performance information in real time and regulate content material therefore.

For instance, if a pupil struggles with a selected math concept, the AI gadget can provide extra sporting events, explanatory movies, or interactive simulations. Conversely, advanced students can access more difficult material, making sure non-stop engagement.

AI-driven tutoring structures offer college students with on-call for help, offering motives and exercise sporting activities on every occasion wanted. Chatbots powered by means of herbal language processing (NLP) can answer not unusual questions, endorse look at substances, and manual students thru complicated topics.

AI tutors bridge the distance between lecture room instruction and impartial look at, making sure that scholars receive non-stop aid outdoor of college hours.

Smart classrooms contain rising technologies together with augmented reality (AR), digital fact (VR), and gamification to make mastering extra engaging and interactive.

AR and VR technologies permit students to explore subjects in ways that traditional strategies can not.

• Virtual area trips: Students can go to ancient sites, discover the sun gadget, or behavior digital technology experiments.

• Medical and engineering simulations: Medical college students can exercise surgical techniques using VR, even as engineering students can design and take a look at systems in a digital surroundings.

• Language gaining knowledge of enhancement: AR-primarily based translation gear help college students analyze new languages thru immersive experiences.

These technologies create attractive, fingers-on learning reviews that enhance know-how retention and information.

Gamification applies recreation-layout factors to academic settings to decorate motivation and participation. AI-driven educational video games reward college students for progress, provide immediately remarks, and adapt difficulty levels primarily based on overall performance.

For example, AI-based totally language getting to know apps like Duolingo use gamification to encourage non-stop getting to know thru factors, badges, and development monitoring.

By making getting to know fun and interactive, gamification improves scholar engagement and fosters a deeper understanding of complicated subjects.

While clever classrooms offer numerous benefits, they also present several challenges and moral concerns that must be addressed:

Not all college students have same get right of entry to to AI-pushed academic era. Socioeconomic disparities can limit get right of entry to to smart classrooms, creating an academic gap between privileged and underserved groups. Ensuring widespread access to AI-powered studying equipment is vital for academic equity.

AI-driven academic structures collect enormous quantities of pupil data, elevating worries about privacy and safety. Schools and establishments should enforce strict statistics protection measures to guard pupil data and save you unauthorized use.

While AI enhances efficiency, it cannot replace the human connection between teachers and college students. Emotional intelligence, mentorship, and social interaction remain important aspects of training. The task lies in integrating AI in a way that supports, in place of replaces, the human element of teaching.

AI structures must gain knowledge of on various datasets to keep away from biases which could have an effect on educational effects. If now not nicely managed, AI algorithms can beef up existing inequalities, favoring positive groups over others.

As AI and educational generation keep to adapt, the future of smart classrooms will likely consist of:

• AI-pushed holographic teachers that offer real-time education.

• Blockchain-primarily based credentialing to make certain steady and verifiable instructional records.

• Neural interface mastering that integrates AI without delay with brainwave activity for enhanced cognition.

• Autonomous AI teaching assistants that help educators with real-time insights and automated lesson planning.

The purpose of clever lecture rooms isn't always to update traditional education but to beautify it through supplying customized, efficient, and attractive mastering reviews.

Smart school rooms and AI-driven instructional technology are reworking the getting to know enjoy through personalizing instruction, improving engagement, and automating administrative duties. While those advancements offer enormous blessings, challenges associated with accessibility, privateness, and the evolving role of educators ought to be addressed. The destiny of schooling lies in striking a balance among generation and human interplay, making sure that AI complements instead of replaces conventional teaching techniques.

CHAPTER 4

Ethical and Social Dimensions of AI in Education

4.1. Ethical Issues in Education with AI

The integration of Artificial Intelligence (AI) into schooling increases severa ethical worries that must be addressed to make sure that this technological development is both useful and truthful. The ability of AI to revolutionize training is gigantic, however it additionally comes with dangers that would impact college students, educators, and society as an entire.

One of the maximum pressing moral troubles associated with AI in education is bias. AI structures are educated on big datasets, and if these datasets include biased statistics, the AI can inadvertently perpetuate or even enlarge those biases. For example, if AI structures used for grading or assessment depend upon biased information that favor sure demographic agencies, college students from underrepresented groups can also face unfair risks. This ought to lead to disparities in instructional outcomes and undermine the ideas of equality and equity that training systems try to uphold.

Moreover, biases in AI can have an effect on not handiest grading but additionally personalized gaining knowledge of. AI algorithms that examine student overall performance and propose tailor-made getting to know assets might also by accident prioritize content that reflects sure cultural, socio-monetary, or gender biases. It is vital for educators, policymakers, and AI developers to collaborate in addressing these issues by means of making sure that training datasets are numerous, representative, and loose from biases that could negatively have an effect on vulnerable scholar populations.

Another full-size ethical problem is privacy. AI technology in education often require the gathering and evaluation of huge amounts of private statistics to create customized gaining knowledge of reports. This data might also include touchy statistics approximately a scholar's academic history, behavior, fitness, or even social interactions. The good sized series of such data increases worries about the safety and privateness of scholar records.

Schools and educational establishments ought to make sure that they're transparent about how student information is accrued, saved, and used. There should be clean pointers on consent, and students (and their guardians) should be absolutely knowledgeable approximately what statistics is being amassed and how it is going to be used. In addition, strong cybersecurity measures should be put in location to defend this data from unauthorized access or breaches, as touchy statistics will be exploited if uncovered.

AI's capacity to monitor and track pupil progress in actual-time additionally creates questions on surveillance. While real-time feedback can be useful for personalized getting to know, there may be a first-class line among presenting useful insights and infringing on students' autonomy and privateness.

Striking the proper balance among information-driven schooling and person privacy is important to ensuring that AI technologies are used ethically in educational settings.

As AI turns into extra embedded in academic environments, there are questions about the position of instructors. Some argue that AI should replace human instructors or decrease their authority in the lecture room. While AI can assist in automating administrative obligations, grading, and offering personalised getting to know assets, the position of a instructor in guiding students, supplying emotional support, and fostering social interaction stays irreplaceable.

The ethical question here revolves around how AI can complement and help instructors with out undermining their role inside the instructional process. AI ought to be regarded as a device that empowers instructors, helping them to awareness greater on higher-stage duties including student engagement and essential thinking, instead of a replacement for the trainer-pupil dating. Educators ought to be concerned inside the implementation of AI inside the study room to make certain that it complements, in preference to replaces, their instructional practices.

The implementation of AI in education may exacerbate current inequalities. While AI has the capacity to provide personalized mastering experiences and guide college students with diverse needs, it additionally requires giant funding in technology and infrastructure. Schools in wealthier regions might also have get right of entry to to advanced AI-powered academic gear, even as faculties in underfunded or marginalized groups may not.

This digital divide creates an moral quandary, as unequal get entry to to AI-primarily based educational resources should result in in addition disparities in instructional first-class. Students in deprived regions won't enjoy the identical possibilities as their wealthier friends, widening the success hole. To mitigate this, governments, educators, and tech agencies must work collectively to ensure equitable get entry to to AI-powered gear and educational assets for all college students, regardless of their socio-economic history.

AI's role in training additionally increases concerns about scholar autonomy and the capability for over-reliance on era. As AI systems offer tailor-made getting to know reports, there is a threat that students can also end up too dependent on era to guide their getting to know, leading to a lack of self-motivation, crucial wondering, and hassle-solving competencies. Education must aim to foster impartial notion, creativity, and lifetime getting to know, instead of developing passive rookies who depend solely on AI structures to determine what and how they learn.

To deal with this problem, it is vital to make certain that AI gear do not overshadow the significance of human agency in the gaining knowledge of manner. Students ought to be endorsed to suppose significantly about the content supplied to them via AI structures and to actively interact with academic materials. AI can guide studying, however it ought to in no way update the position of college students in riding their very own schooling.

The moral implications of AI in schooling also make bigger to the design and implementation system. As AI technologies are incorporated into educational settings, it's miles important that they may be reachable, inclusive, and designed with the desires of all college students in thoughts. AI tools have to now not prefer sure mastering styles, disabilities, or cultural backgrounds at the same time as neglecting others.

Inclusive layout is prime to making sure that AI technology paintings for everyone, including students with disabilities. For instance, AI tools can be used to provide textual content-to-speech functionality for visually impaired college students or adjust getting to know materials for students with mastering disabilities. However, the improvement of AI gear ought to contain diverse groups who can perceive and deal with the wishes of all student populations to save you the era from inadvertently apart from or disadvantaging positive groups.

Lastly, there may be the query of the long-time period moral effect of AI in training. As AI continues to adapt and will become greater advanced, it is able to result in significant adjustments inside the manner society views education. Will AI-pushed schooling cause a extra knowledgeable and capable society, or will it toughen present social and monetary divides? Will it beautify human capacity, or will it decrease human agency and creativity?

These are crucial questions that require cautious attention. Ethical frameworks for AI in training have to account for the capability long-term results of the era and strive to create a future in which AI helps and enriches human getting to know, in preference to diminishing the human experience.

The moral problems surrounding AI in education are complex and multifaceted, encompassing concerns approximately bias, privacy, trainer roles, get right of entry to, autonomy, equity, and the long-term impact of generation. As AI continues to form the destiny of education, it's far important that these moral considerations are addressed in a way that promotes equity, inclusivity, and the well-being of all college students. By taking a thoughtful, collaborative approach to the integration of AI, we are able to make certain that this effective device is used responsibly and efficaciously to decorate the getting to know enjoy for generations to return.

4.2. AI and Student Privacy

Artificial intelligence (AI) is reworking education, however it also brings huge ethical issues regarding scholar privacy. As AI systems grow to be increasingly integrated into instructional environments, big quantities of pupil facts are being amassed, processed, and stored, elevating questions on the safety of private statistics.

AI systems in training depend upon amassing great quantities of scholar statistics to customise mastering experiences. To offer tailored content material and comments, AI equipment frequently require distinctive records approximately college students' instructional history, examination results, behavioral facts, and every now and then even social interactions. The number one goal is to create individualized getting to know pathways that assist college students succeed, however this comes on the cost of potentially compromising privateness.

The advantages of information series in instructional AI are simple; but, the risks to privacy are tremendous. Personal facts, together with academic records, behavioral styles, and even biometric data, can turn out to be liable to unauthorized access and misuse. Educational institutions ought to make certain that explicit, knowledgeable consent is obtained from students before their information is accumulated and used. Additionally, AI developers should be transparent about how they take care of pupil statistics and adhere to strict information protection policies to keep away from misuse.

One of the important thing blessings of AI in education is its ability to constantly screen student learning and behavior. AI structures can song a student's participation in classes, examination overall performance, getting to know velocity, or even their interactions with the content material. This information is precious for optimizing gaining knowledge of studies, identifying students' strengths and weaknesses, and offering targeted support.

However, continuous monitoring increases worries about student privateness. The constant statement of students' behavior ought to make them sense like they are being scrutinized or judged, which may cause discomfort or tension. The concept of "always being watched" may stifle students' capability to examine freely, as the know-how that their every movement is being recorded can be psychologically taxing. The ability for invasive surveillance poses a challenge to retaining a healthful mastering surroundings where college students experience secure and motivated to interact of their research.

Ensuring the security of pupil statistics is paramount when the usage of AI in schooling. Personal statistics amassed by way of AI systems should be saved securely, included from unauthorized get right of entry to, and treated with the utmost confidentiality. Given that many educational structures are cloud-based totally, scholar information is saved on outside servers, which makes it liable to cyberattacks and statistics breaches. It is vital that academic establishments enforce strong cybersecurity measures to protect the privateness of pupil facts.

Moreover, AI developers ought to observe strict protocols to guard records each in transit and at relaxation. Encryption, get entry to manipulate, and regular protection audits are critical in stopping unauthorized access and making sure that touchy information stays covered. Institutions should additionally offer college students with transparency approximately how their facts is being used and what protections are in area to keep it steady.

Another ethical challenge in AI schooling is the unauthorized use of scholar data. While the purpose of AI structures is to personalize studying and enhance instructional outcomes, there may be a danger that information will be exploited for industrial functions or used in approaches that were not at the start supposed. For instance, pupil statistics is probably bought to third parties, or used for targeted advertising, which could undermine the privacy of students.

To mitigate those risks, it's miles crucial that educational AI systems are designed to prioritize privateness. Student information need to handiest be used for educational functions and should not be shared with out express consent. Additionally, AI structures have to be obvious approximately their statistics utilization rules, and students need to be given manipulate over their non-public records, consisting of the capacity to decide out of statistics series or request deletion of their statistics.

The steady tracking enabled through AI in training may also have psychological results on students. Knowing that their every pass, solution, and interplay is being recorded can create anxiety and have an effect on students' mental nicely-being. Students may additionally experience as even though they're below consistent evaluation, that could negatively impact their getting to know experience.

Furthermore, this surveillance could cause a reduction in students' autonomy and self-self belief. When college students feel that their privateness is being invaded, they'll turn out to be much less willing to explicit themselves freely in the school room, restricting their potential to learn and develop. The strain to perform for an AI gadget rather than a human trainer may discourage chance-taking and creativity, which can be important aspects of studying.

As AI will become greater embedded in education, it's far crucial to establish moral tips that protect scholar privacy. Educational establishments, AI builders, and policymakers have to work collectively to create a framework that guarantees the responsible use of AI while respecting students' privacy rights. These pointers ought to outline how student records is accumulated, stored, and shared, in addition to the measures taken to guard it from misuse.

AI builders have to additionally put in force privacy by way of layout standards in their structures, which means that privacy concerns are integrated into the development method from the outset. Transparency and responsibility are key additives of this approach. Students ought to be knowledgeable approximately how their information is used and need to have manipulate over their personal information. Furthermore, institutions have to provide college students with the ability to get right of entry to, alter, or delete their information in the event that they wish to achieve this.

While AI has the capacity to revolutionize education, it's miles vital that the privacy of college students is safeguarded within the system. As AI structures increasingly more collect and system student data, concerns about privacy, protection, and the moral use of data will keep growing. Educational establishments and AI builders have to be vigilant in shielding student privacy and ensuring that AI is used responsibly. By prioritizing transparency, protection, and pupil consent, AI can be harnessed to enhance training with out compromising the privacy rights of college students.

4.3. AI and the Teacher-Student Relationship

The integration of artificial intelligence (AI) in training has brought great changes to the dynamics of teaching and getting to know. One of the most profound transformations is the way wherein AI is reshaping the connection among instructors and college students. While AI can beautify instructional reviews with the aid of imparting customized learning and administrative assist, it additionally increases questions about the nature of human connection, the function of educators, and the impact at the emotional and social aspects of studying.

As AI tools end up more extensive in educational settings, the role of instructors is transferring. In many approaches, AI is taking on obligations that were once solely managed by teachers, which includes grading assignments, tracking student development, and providing instant comments. These technology permit teachers to dedicate greater time to fostering essential questioning, creativity, and interpersonal capabilities, regions that AI isn't always yet able to addressing efficaciously.

AI has the capacity to assist instructors by way of automating administrative duties, providing insights into student performance, and offering personalised learning pathways for college kids. For example, AI-powered getting to know control systems can monitor students' development in real time, discover areas wherein they're struggling, and endorse targeted interventions. This records permits teachers to attention their attention on the individual desires of college students, for this reason improving the overall mastering experience. Teachers can spend more time enticing with students in a significant way, supporting them navigate complicated thoughts and fostering a deeper expertise of the concern count.

However, as AI takes on more duties, some educators fear that their position becomes much less non-public and greater mechanized. The feel of connection that comes from human interaction—whether it's imparting encouragement, supplying emotional support, or adjusting teaching techniques to house diverse getting to know patterns—might also lessen as AI gear emerge as more normal. Teachers may also locate themselves relying on technology greater than on their personal instincts and understanding in their students. The ability for dehumanizing the educational revel in is a sizeable situation, specifically in environments wherein personal relationships are important to student achievement.

Rather than replacing instructors, AI must be regarded as a complementary device that complements their potential to engage with college students. AI can manage repetitive responsibilities, such as administrative paintings, whilst teachers awareness at the personal, emotional, and social factors of coaching. For example, AI-powered tutoring structures can offer extra support for college students out of doors the school room, imparting personalized explanations and exercise physical activities. This can unfastened up teachers to engage in greater meaningful face-to-face interactions with college students, addressing their unique worries and imparting steering in areas that require human empathy and understanding.

In this situation, the instructor-scholar courting can evolve into one in which instructors turn out to be facilitators of learning, guiding students via complicated ideas and fostering an surroundings of collaboration and crucial thinking. AI can offer the foundational knowledge and guide, while instructors cognizance on nurturing interest, creativity, and emotional intelligence—skills which are vital for college kids' common improvement. By operating along AI, teachers can provide a greater tailored and human-targeted instructional experience that balances technology with human connection.

While AI can beautify the educational revel in in many ways, it additionally introduces the risk of emotional disconnect. The maximum large issue approximately AI's function in training is the capacity for lowering the human factor of teaching. Education isn't always pretty much transferring expertise; it's also about building consider, empathy, and rapport. Teachers play a important function in helping students experience valued and understood, which could appreciably effect their learning results.

AI, by means of its nature, lacks emotional intelligence. While AI structures may be programmed to reply to students' queries and adapt to their gaining knowledge of wishes, they can not provide the emotional support that a teacher can offer. The ability to provide encouragement throughout moments of conflict, to apprehend the emotional needs of college students, and to foster a experience of belonging is an important part of powerful coaching. AI cannot replicate the human qualities that make these interactions significant.

For instance, when a pupil is feeling discouraged, they might need extra than simply instructional assist; they want empathy, reassurance, and customized encouragement. AI lacks the ability to apprehend those emotional cues and reply in a way that fosters connection. This creates the danger that scholars may additionally feel isolated or alienated, specially in conditions wherein emotional or mental assist is needed maximum.

To mitigate the emotional disconnect that AI may additionally introduce, it is critical that educators prioritize human interplay in their classrooms. While AI can handle the various technical aspects of education, the role of the teacher in fostering relationships with students have to continue to be valuable. Teachers need to maintain to have interaction with students on an emotional and social stage, providing guidance and help that AI can't mirror.

Teachers can use AI as a tool to assist perceive when a pupil can be suffering academically, however it's miles still up to the instructor to cope with the pupil's emotional needs. By keeping open communication, growing a supportive study room environment, and fostering an ecosystem of mutual appreciate, instructors can make certain that scholars sense connected and valued, even in a technology-pushed lecture room. AI must no longer replace the human element of coaching however must decorate the ability of instructors to satisfy the numerous desires of their students.

Moreover, it's far important for educators to receive training in the usage of AI tools successfully. Teachers need to be equipped with the knowledge and capabilities to leverage AI without losing sight of the personal connections which are vital to the academic manner. They need to learn to apply AI to complement their teaching, offering a balanced method that combines the performance of technology with the warmth and empathy that only human educators can provide.

The increasing reliance on AI in training also increases ethical questions on the role of technology in trainer-student interactions. As AI structures gather records on students' behaviors, performance, and even emotions, questions rise up about who owns this information and how it is used. There is a want for transparency and consent in relation to amassing and making use of pupil data, and instructors ought to be privy to the moral implications of using AI tools that acquire personal statistics.

Furthermore, AI's ability to persuade teacher-scholar dynamics also increases worries approximately fairness and bias. If AI systems aren't cautiously designed, they will strengthen present biases or perpetuate inequalities in education. For example, AI algorithms may additionally inadvertently prefer positive student populations or offer biased hints based totally on incomplete or skewed data. Teachers should be vigilant in ensuring that AI is used ethically and that it does now not perpetuate or exacerbate educational disparities.

The trainer-pupil relationship is evolving in the age of AI, with technology playing an more and more primary function in shaping how schooling is introduced and skilled. While AI offers valuable gear for boosting gaining knowledge of and helping teachers, it also introduces new demanding situations associated with emotional connection, ethical issues, and the stability between technology and human interaction. Teachers should keep to play an active function in fostering non-public relationships with students, ensuring that the human element of schooling remains intact. By the usage of AI to complement rather than update their coaching, educators can create an enriched mastering surroundings that mixes the nice of both worlds: the power of generation and the warmth of human connection.

4.4. Data Governance and Security in AI Education

In the swiftly evolving subject of AI-pushed education, statistics governance and safety have emerged as pivotal issues.

As educational establishments and era companies increasingly more integrate AI structures into teaching, assessment, and administrative capabilities, extensive amounts of facts are generated, accrued, and analyzed. This includes sensitive private records, getting to know behavior analytics, biometric data, and overall performance statistics. The control of this facts raises profound questions on privacy, moral use, ownership, get entry to, and the long-time period implications of algorithmic selection-making.

Data governance in AI training refers back to the guidelines, standards, approaches, and technologies used to manipulate facts's availability, usability, integrity, and security. These governance structures ensure that information is treated responsibly and complies with applicable prison and ethical frameworks. Security, however, focuses extra on protecting that data from unauthorized get entry to, corruption, or theft. Together, they shape the spine of a truthful virtual mastering environment.

The first primary attention on this area is the possession of scholar records. With AI platforms often provided through 1/3-birthday celebration companies, questions arise about who controls the records accumulated via those systems. Does the statistics belong to the pupil, the group, or the agency growing the AI device? Clear regulatory frameworks are critical to keep away from exploitation or misuse. Initiatives just like the General Data Protection Regulation (GDPR) in Europe and the Family Educational Rights and Privacy Act (FERPA) inside the United States provide a few legal scaffolding, but the worldwide nature of online education necessitates a more harmonized method.

Secondly, facts privateness is an pressing trouble. AI systems thrive on massive datasets to examine and enhance their fashions. However, the inclusion of individually identifiable records (PII) together with names, grades, conduct logs, and from time to time even audio-visual facts raises great privacy worries. Robust anonymization strategies, differential privacy fashions, and federated mastering processes are being explored as solutions to mitigate these dangers at the same time as maintaining the utility of the facts for AI algorithms.

Thirdly, bias and fairness in AI-driven educational choices hinge at the satisfactory and governance of records. Poorly curated or non-consultant records can cause biased algorithms that unfairly drawback certain college students. For instance, AI-based totally grading or customized gaining knowledge of paths can also inadvertently reflect socioeconomic, racial, or gender biases gift inside the historical records. Effective facts governance need to consequently consist of continuous auditing, bias detection protocols, and the inclusion of various datasets to promote fairness.

Security threats also loom big. Educational establishments are increasingly turning into objectives for cyberattacks because of their widespread repositories of touchy information. AI structures, while improving operational efficiency, can also introduce new vulnerabilities. For instance, adversarial attacks on machine studying fashions may want to manipulate results which includes grades or tips. Ensuring strong cybersecurity infrastructure, consisting of encryption, multi-factor authentication, and intrusion detection structures, is critical for maintaining agree with in AI-more suitable schooling.

Furthermore, transparency and explainability are imperative to moral data governance. Students and educators need to apprehend how AI structures attain their conclusions—whether in grading, comments, or curriculum adjustments. Black-box models that do not offer interpretability can erode trust and obstruct meaningful oversight. As such, incorporating explainable AI (XAI) frameworks and maintaining transparent records usage logs are an increasing number of seen as high-quality practices.

Another measurement includes statistics retention and lifecycle management. Educational information might also maintain to maintain private cost long after a direction has concluded. Governance rules have to define how lengthy information is retained, whilst it's miles deleted, and beneath what situations it may be reused. This requires dynamic consent models that allow students to manage their records possibilities over the years, inclusive of options to revoke get right of entry to.

A key enabler of sturdy records governance is the advent of interdisciplinary information ethics boards inside instructional institutions. These our bodies, composed of educators, technologists, felony experts, and students, can oversee the implementation of statistics policies, compare supplier partnerships, and mediate disputes. Their role ensures that records governance aligns now not only with technical and prison standards but also with the organization's instructional values and assignment.

Additionally, scholar empowerment and virtual literacy are fundamental. Learners need to be knowledgeable about their statistics rights, the results of facts sharing, and the functioning of AI structures they have interaction with. Such attention fosters knowledgeable consent and encourages greater energetic participation in discussions approximately AI ethics in training.

In the worldwide context, move-border statistics drift offers a new layer of complexity. Many AI academic equipment operate globally, and facts can be stored in special jurisdictions. Harmonizing facts governance practices throughout borders might be important, specially in ensuring that scholars from growing countries or underrepresented groups are not subjected to exploitative practices due to weaker neighborhood regulations.

Looking ahead, blockchain and decentralized identification systems may also offer novel strategies to information governance. Blockchain can provide immutable records of information access and changes, empowering students with manipulate over who sees and makes use of their instructional facts. Such improvements, even as nonetheless nascent, should redefine agree with in instructional records control.

Data governance and security in AI education aren't simply technical demanding situations—they are moral imperatives that form the destiny of studying. As AI maintains to permeate instructional environments, establishments ought to spend money on resilient governance frameworks, strong security structures, and obvious communication techniques. Only by means of doing so can we construct an academic environment that respects privateness, promotes fairness, and prepares rookies for a digitally pushed international.

4.5. Addressing Equity and Access in AI Implementations

Artificial Intelligence (AI) has the transformative ability to reshape training by using tailoring mastering experiences, growing operational performance, and supporting educators in handing over extra impactful coaching. However, as AI technologies emerge as an increasing number of embedded inside academic structures, worries around fairness and get entry to have emerged as giant and pressing problems. Without intentional design and implementation, AI can perpetuate or maybe exacerbate present disparities in training.

Access to AI-powered instructional gear relies upon closely on digital infrastructure, which includes dependable net, modern-day gadgets, and technical assist. Many underserved groups, mainly in rural or economically disadvantaged areas, lack those foundational elements. Students in such regions won't have private gadgets or strong internet connections, proscribing their capability to benefit from AI systems designed to supply personalized instruction or actual-time feedback.

The disparity turns into particularly glaring in remote gaining knowledge of eventualities. During the COVID-19 pandemic, as an example, millions of college students have been left in the back of due to inadequate virtual get admission to. AI-powered platforms that adapt to person progress or mastering patterns are useless if students can't get admission to them always. Furthermore, many AI equipment are optimized for more moderen hardware, leaving those with previous gadgets not able to make use of advanced features, along with immersive simulations or real-time language translation.

Bridging the virtual divide isn't always completely about device distribution—it additionally calls for funding in infrastructure, inclusive of network Wi-Fi projects, affordable broadband get admission to, and on-site technical help.

Without such measures, the blessings of AI in schooling will stay disproportionately skewed toward the digitally privileged.

AI systems are only as right because the facts they're educated on. When datasets are skewed or non-consultant, AI fashions can produce biased or culturally insensitive results. This issue is mainly troubling in instructional contexts where fairness and equity are paramount.

For example, AI algorithms used for automatic grading or student profiling may be trained predominantly on information from precise linguistic or cultural backgrounds. This may want to disadvantage students from minority groups, whose dialects, communique patterns, or studying behaviors may not align with the records patterns the set of rules acknowledges. Similarly, recommendation engines that guide college students towards publications or profession paths would possibly support existing societal inequalities if historical records displays systemic biases—together with underrepresentation of women in STEM fields.

To deal with this, builders should audit training datasets for range and implement bias mitigation strategies, which includes antagonistic education, fairness-conscious modeling, and continuous validation across demographic corporations. Additionally, enticing educators, community leaders, and students from underrepresented businesses within the layout and testing of AI systems ensures that the resulting technologies are more culturally responsive and inclusive.

Another layer of inequality stems from the dominance of English in AI schooling equipment. While English is a worldwide language of technology, thousands and thousands of learners have interaction in education via nearby or indigenous languages. AI structures that can not understand or generate content material in those languages inherently marginalize non-English-speaking rookies.

Machine translation has made sizeable advances, but nuances in grammar, idioms, and cultural context can nonetheless lead to misinterpretations or irrelevant content shipping. Moreover, voice reputation and natural language processing models often carry out poorly for accents or dialects which can be underrepresented in schooling statistics, which could have an effect on speech-primarily based tutoring systems or interactive AI assistants.

Creating AI tools that support multilingualism calls for investment in developing first-rate corpora in underrepresented languages and in schooling AI fashions on numerous linguistic datasets. Additionally, localized content—not simply translated content material—must be advanced to mirror the cultural and pedagogical wishes of various learners. By doing so, AI can foster greater equitable get entry to to know-how across linguistic limitations.

The commercialization of AI in schooling affords any other project to equity. Many high-acting AI getting to know systems are developed by private corporations and come with subscription models, licensing charges, or charges for top class features. Schools and students in low-earnings regions may be not able to have enough money these equipment, in addition deepening instructional inequality.

Even in public education systems, the adoption of AI technology can be restricted by way of budgetary constraints. Decisions approximately which faculties or districts get hold of AI investments often reflect current funding inequalities, resulting in a tiered schooling machine where wealthier establishments have get right of entry to to modern-day gear and others depend upon previous methods.

To combat this, governments, NGOs, and philanthropic corporations should prioritize equitable investment fashions that make sure customary access to AI equipment. Open-source tasks and public-non-public partnerships can play a essential position in democratizing get right of entry to, making effective AI-driven educational assets freely to be had or low priced at scale. Additionally, encouraging opposition and innovation among startups focused on low-value AI answers can help stage the gambling field.

AI structures in training need to also accommodate students with disabilities or learning variations. While AI holds promise for adaptive gaining knowledge of and personalized aid, many current gear aren't designed with typical accessibility in thoughts. For instance, AI systems may additionally lack aid for display screen readers, voice manipulate, or alternative input techniques, making them hard to use for students with visual, auditory, or motor impairments.

AI-pushed mastering structures have to comply with generic design ideas from the outset, incorporating accessibility standards which includes WCAG (Web Content Accessibility Guidelines). Furthermore, AI can actively beautify accessibility—as an instance, by producing actual-time captions, providing textual content-to-speech features, or customizing person interfaces primarily based on unique getting to know desires.

Collaborating with accessibility experts, incapacity advocates, and inclusive training specialists all through the layout and testing levels is crucial to ensure that AI gear do not inadvertently exclude college students with disabilities. When nicely implemented, AI has the potential to significantly expand possibilities for rookies who have traditionally faced limitations to schooling.

Ensuring fairness in AI schooling implementations calls for sturdy moral frameworks and coverage interventions. Policymakers have to proactively alter the deployment of AI to save you exacerbation of inequality. This includes mandating transparency in algorithmic choice-making, implementing data privateness protections, and requiring fairness effect checks before big-scale implementation.

Educational establishments ought to also establish inner regulations around facts usage, scholar consent, and algorithmic duty. Importantly, equity ought to be a primary criterion in procurement choices—equipment that lack accessibility functions, bias audits, or multilingual support must not be followed at scale.

Moreover, ethics forums, composed of educators, college students, ethicists, and community representatives, can provide oversight and assist establishments navigate the complicated trade-offs involved in AI adoption. These forums have to have the authority to pause or reject AI implementations that pose dangers to marginalized groups.

Finally, addressing equity in AI training isn't entirely a technical or coverage hassle—it's also a social one. Meaningful inclusion of the groups maximum suffering from educational inequality is crucial. This manner regarding students, mother and father, teachers, and network leaders in the development, trying out, and comments cycles of AI gear.

Participatory design practices make certain that AI technology reflect the lived reviews and priorities of numerous novices. Community comments can reveal blind spots in algorithmic design, discover unintended results, and guide more equitable deployment strategies. Moreover, whilst groups experience possession over the technology they use, adoption and effectiveness enhance.

Educational establishments should foster transparency about how AI systems paintings and provide education to assist stakeholders apprehend their benefits and boundaries. Building virtual literacy and critical wondering round AI among educators and inexperienced persons is essential for equitable and moral use.

AI has the electricity to revolutionize training, but its advantages will continue to be erratically dispensed unless issues of equity and get admission to are addressed with urgency and care. From infrastructural disparities and algorithmic bias to language barriers and affordability, a big selection of demanding situations must be tackled to ensure that AI complements, in preference to hinders, inclusive education.

Designing AI systems via the lens of justice, representation, and accessibility is not merely a ethical vital—it's also crucial for maximizing the impact and effectiveness of these equipment. By centering fairness in policy, practice, and layout, we can construct an educational future wherein AI uplifts all inexperienced persons, regardless of their historical past, identity, or geography.

4.6. The Societal Impact of AI on Future Generations

Artificial Intelligence (AI) stands at the heart of the continued technological revolution, promising to reshape nearly every factor of human lifestyles. For destiny generations, AI isn't always simply a device; it is an fundamental a part of their environment, embedded in educational structures, social systems, economies, and cultural frameworks. As such, its societal effect is profound and multi-dimensional, influencing how individuals develop, examine, communicate, work, and understand the world. Understanding those implications is important to ensuring that AI serves as a pressure for equitable development in preference to exacerbating present disparities or growing new moral dilemmas.

One of the most distinguished approaches in which AI is anticipated to effect destiny generations is through the transformation of the hard work market. Traditional activity structures are hastily changing due to automation and gadget gaining knowledge of structures capable of acting complex duties once reserved for people. While AI opens up new fields and possibilities—including AI ethics consulting, prompt engineering, and shrewd gadget layout—it also renders a few roles obsolete. Future generations should adapt to an economy where cognitive flexibility, creativity, and emotional intelligence come to be as vital as technical understanding. The idea of lifelong gaining knowledge of is not aspirational but important, and societies have to support non-stop ability improvement to make sure that people remain applicable and effective in AI-greater workplaces.

The reconfiguration of schooling systems via AI additionally plays a imperative function in shaping societal norms and values. AI-powered systems now provide customized getting to know pathways that modify in real time to pupil desires. These structures promise to democratize get entry to to pleasant schooling, but in addition they threat entrenching inequality if access is erratically allotted. Children growing up in beneath-resourced regions can also discover themselves similarly marginalized if they lack connectivity, virtual literacy, or access to AI-better educational tools. The destiny of training, therefore, hinges on making sure inclusivity and establishing infrastructure that presents all college students same access to AI's benefits.

Beyond education and work, AI will impact how destiny generations shape relationships and have interaction socially. The integration of AI in verbal exchange systems, social media algorithms, and even companionship technologies like conversational agents and robotic pets will redefine human interplay. For virtual natives raised in AI-mediated environments, identification formation and social belonging might also arise thru unique paradigms than previous generations. This shift introduces each opportunities and challenges: even as AI can aid intellectual health through digital remedy gear and beautify connectivity, it is able to also foster echo chambers, filter out bubbles, and a decline in real human connection if no longer carefully managed.

Culturally, AI's role as a co-creator of artwork, literature, and song reshapes the limits of human expression. Future generations will develop up in a international in which a number of their favorite songs, testimonies, or artistic endeavors are generated no longer via humans however with the aid of algorithms trained on large datasets of human creativity. This increases questions about authenticity, ownership, and the fee of human labor. At the identical time, it gives an accelerated canvas for expression—AI can come to be a partner in creativity, improving in preference to replacing the human creativeness. Educational establishments and cultural frameworks must adapt to manual younger human beings in understanding, comparing, and leveraging AI as a device in inventive endeavors.

The mental and cognitive development of future generations may also be molded by way of AI's ubiquity. Children uncovered to shrewd systems from early early life—along with digital assistants, AI toys, and personalized academic content material—might also develop distinctive approaches of processing statistics, fixing troubles, and tasty with the arena. Some researchers speculate that those interactions could have an effect on attention spans, crucial thinking talents, or emotional intelligence. There is also difficulty about surveillance and autonomy; children raised in environments saturated with tracking and behavior-shaping technology may internalize surveillance as normative, affecting their perceptions of privateness, freedom, and consider.

From a societal perspective, possibly one of the maximum massive worries lies in the ethical frameworks that govern AI improvement and deployment. Future generations will inherit not simplest the capabilities of AI however also the biases, limitations, and ethical selections embedded inside it. Algorithms skilled on ancient statistics frequently mirror and extend societal prejudices, main to discriminatory effects in regions such as policing, hiring, healthcare, and education. If unchecked, these styles can perpetuate systemic inequality below the guise of goal choice-making. As such, cultivating AI literacy and ethical consciousness among young humans will become paramount. They must be empowered to impeach, audit, and reshape the structures that shape them.

AI's have an effect on on governance and civic engagement is another location with far-reaching outcomes. With AI more and more hired in coverage modeling, predictive policing, public provider optimization, and electoral strategies, destiny citizens will need to have interaction critically with algorithmic governance. The capability for technocracy—in which choices are made with the aid of statistics-driven structures as opposed to democratic deliberation—necessitates robust civic education to put together kids to participate meaningfully in democratic societies. Transparency, responsibility, and participatory layout methods must be institutionalized to prevent disenfranchisement in the call of performance.

The environmental implications of AI improvement also intersect with the values and priorities of future generations. As focus of climate exchange intensifies, younger cohorts are already vocal approximately sustainability and planetary stewardship. However, the training of large AI fashions consumes giant amounts of electricity and water. Future technologists should confront the ecological fee of innovation and prioritize inexperienced AI—systems designed with environmental sustainability in thoughts. Encouraging interdisciplinary schooling that combines AI with ecology, ethics, and systems wondering can prepare future leaders to navigate this complex terrain.

Religion, philosophy, and spirituality will even stumble upon shifts as AI keeps to blur the boundaries among human and gadget. Questions about consciousness, business enterprise, and the soul will flow from speculative fiction into public discourse. Young human beings will grapple with what it means to be human in an age of artificial minds. Will AI partners be granted rights? Can a system be creative, empathetic, or ethical? These questions venture deeply held beliefs and invite reexamination of human exceptionalism.

The societal effect of AI on future generations is both expansive and profound. While AI holds monstrous potential to beautify human existence, it also poses dangers that must be carefully navigated. Education structures, households, governments, and developers share a collective duty to shape a future in which AI empowers instead of alienates. Future generations must no longer be passive recipients of AI's influence, but active co-creators of its role in society. This calls for equipping them with the gear, information, and moral grounding to interact significantly with intelligent systems—and to examine futures wherein generation serves humanity's maximum ideals.

4.7. Human Oversight and Accountability in AI Systems

As artificial intelligence structures an increasing number of permeate education, healthcare, governance, and the non-public sector, the call for for clear frameworks ensuring human oversight and duty has turn out to be paramount. While AI offers transformative ability, it also poses large ethical, social, and operational dangers if left unchecked. In the context of schooling particularly, where choices can effect the cognitive development, emotional nicely-being, and future possibilities of newbies, the presence of human judgment stays irreplaceable. Oversight and accountability, then, aren't ancillary concerns—they're foundational to the accountable implementation of AI.

The precept of human oversight refers to the need that humans remain on top of things of, or at least meaningfully worried with, AI systems. This can include supervision, approval, or the capability to override selections made via algorithms. Accountability, alternatively, implies that identifiable people or institutions are held accountable for AI-pushed consequences, ensuring transparency in how decisions are made and permitting corrective measures whilst mistakes or damage arise.

One of the essential motives for human oversight is the non-deterministic nature of system gaining knowledge of fashions. These structures frequently characteristic as black bins, deriving conclusions based on styles in statistics that aren't constantly obvious to users. In an academic context, as an example, a pupil is probably flagged as underperforming or disengaged via an AI device, triggering interventions or altering their academic route. Without human oversight, such choices may be based on incomplete, biased, or misinterpreted information—leading to consequences that are not simply erroneous but additionally unjust.

Human oversight mitigates the risks of dehumanization in training. When content transport, assessments, and remarks are automated with out enough trainer involvement, the relational and emotional dimensions of gaining knowledge of are regularly lost. Educators play a critical function in interpreting records, know-how contextual subtleties, and supplying encouragement—features AI cannot replicate authentically. Ensuring that human educators hold the authority to interpret and query AI-generated insights is important for retaining the humanity of schooling.

Equally crucial is organising clean accountability mechanisms for the deployment and effects of AI systems. In many sectors, inclusive of education, a lack of transparency around AI decision-making has caused public mistrust and legal demanding situations. When errors arise—which include misclassifications, discriminatory patterns, or breaches of privateness—there need to be established channels for redress. Schools, developers, and educational authorities must collaborate to decide who is accountable whilst AI fails and the way such failures are documented, audited, and remedied.

To assist this, there's a developing name for explainable AI (XAI), which seeks to make AI structures more obvious by way of providing human-comprehensible rationales for their outputs. In the school room, this will mean that instructors and students can query why a selected advice changed into made or recognize what statistics stimulated a grade proposal. Such transparency fosters believe and enables educators to verify or contest gadget selections, reinforcing the precept of shared judgment as opposed to gadget dominance.

Ethical oversight our bodies also are becoming more not unusual in establishments that deploy AI. These might also encompass inner AI ethics committees, 0.33-birthday party auditing groups, or regulatory government that evaluate structures for fairness, accuracy, and safety. In education, such bodies can screen whether or not AI applications align with pedagogical goals, fairness standards, and information privacy laws. They function a buffer in opposition to both technological determinism and corporate overreach via embedding ethical evaluate techniques into gadget development and deployment.

Furthermore, responsibility structures need to don't forget lengthy-time period effects. AI structures often evolve thru continuous gaining knowledge of, adapting based on new data through the years. This dynamic nature necessitates ongoing tracking and recalibration to save you float from original dreams or moral limitations. Human oversight should as a consequence be non-stop as opposed to episodic, with mechanisms to replace, pause, or retire systems as contexts exchange.

The inclusion of college students and educators in oversight roles is some other vital measurement. Those maximum stricken by AI selections need to have a voice in how such structures are designed, implemented, and evaluated.

Participatory design approaches that invite enter from diverse stakeholders not only yield more equitable structures however additionally distribute responsibility in a more democratic way. Transparency projects—such as AI file cards or algorithmic impact statements—can in addition empower users by means of demystifying how AI capabilities and what it influences.

Legal frameworks are starting to evolve in reaction to these needs. The European Union's Artificial Intelligence Act, as an instance, mandates rigorous oversight and documentation for high-risk AI systems, consisting of the ones used in training. Other jurisdictions are following healthy, recognizing that codified accountability is important to protect public interest. These regulatory actions emphasize that human oversight isn't always genuinely an internal great exercise however a societal expectation with criminal implications.

Finally, the way of life round AI have to change to include humility and vigilance. Overreliance on era, mainly when framed as impartial or infallible, undermines the duty of human actors to remain engaged and important. Training educators, directors, and college students to apprehend AI's boundaries and to workout informed skepticism is just as essential as technical innovation. A subculture of accountability starts offevolved with recognition and is sustained thru communicate, training, and institutional dedication.

The integration of AI into training should proceed with the unwavering recognition that human beings endure final duty for its effect. Oversight and accountability aren't optional—they may be moral imperatives. By centering human judgment, setting up obvious tactics, and retaining non-stop vigilance, we can make certain that AI serves as a tool for empowerment as opposed to an tool of manage. In doing so, we honor the values of schooling and shield the rights and dignity of future generations.

CHAPTER 5

Artificial Intelligence and Accessibility in Education

5.1. Education Accessibility and Opportunities in AI

The integration of Artificial Intelligence (AI) into training guarantees transformative adjustments in phrases of accessibility and opportunities. As the digital divide remains a massive trouble in worldwide schooling structures, AI presents a potential method to bridging gaps and offering equitable get entry to to high-quality mastering reports.

AI's primary position in improving accessibility lies in its capability to customise and tailor educational studies to the character needs of students. In regions where access to certified educators or good enough academic sources is limited, AI can step in to offer a greater constant and adaptable learning surroundings. AI-driven systems can analyze a scholar's progress, studying style, and precise demanding situations, making an allowance for extra custom designed mastering plans that make sure each learner's wishes are met.

One of the most critical components of enhancing accessibility via AI is its capability to provide training in remote and underserved areas. AI-powered structures, together with digital school rooms and adaptive mastering environments, can reach students who won't in any other case have access to standard lecture room settings. By removing geographical barriers, AI allows students from all around the global to engage with first-rate instructional content with out the limitations of physical infrastructure. This is mainly beneficial for groups in rural or war-affected areas, in which educational opportunities may be sparse or even non-existent.

Moreover, AI can make a contribution drastically to the inclusivity of schooling by using helping college students with numerous mastering needs. For individuals with disabilities, AI gives quite a number equipment that may help conquer limitations to gaining knowledge of. Text-to-speech and speech-to-textual content technologies, AI-pushed signal language interpreters, and customized studying assistants can cater to students with visible, auditory, or mobility impairments. By making studying more accessible to all, AI guarantees that no student is left in the back of due to physical or cognitive boundaries.

AI's potential to provide equal instructional possibilities extends to college students from deprived socioeconomic backgrounds. Often, those students face demanding situations such as restrained access to gaining knowledge of materials, lack of assist structures, or overcrowded classrooms. AI-based solutions, which include virtual tutors and automated grading structures, can lessen the burden on overworked teachers and ensure that scholars in underserved communities get hold of the attention and aid they need. Furthermore, AI's capacity to scale learning answers means that excellent instructional content can be delivered to huge corporations of students concurrently, without compromising the excellent of the getting to know revel in.

While AI can beautify access to education in lots of methods, it is crucial to bear in mind the capacity dangers and challenges that include its implementation. One of the primary worries is the chance of deepening the virtual divide, specially in international locations or regions wherein technological infrastructure is underdeveloped. Access to the net, gadgets, and AI gear is not frequent, and with out right investment in virtual infrastructure, there is a chance that AI's advantages might be disproportionately felt by means of college students in wealthier or extra technologically advanced areas. Therefore, governments, educational establishments, and tech businesses must work collaboratively to make certain that AI technologies are available to all students, regardless of their socio-economic status or geographic location.

Another mission lies inside the moral implications of AI-powered schooling. While AI can provide valuable insights and customized learning stories, it additionally raises questions about privacy, information safety, and algorithmic biases. Collecting and studying massive amounts of personal records from students ought to doubtlessly divulge them to dangers, along with identity robbery or surveillance. To mitigate these risks, it's miles crucial for AI systems to be designed with strong facts safety measures and transparency in mind.

Additionally, AI algorithms ought to be frequently audited to ensure that they are unfastened from bias and they sell equitable educational possibilities for all students.

Ultimately, the function of AI in education extends some distance beyond simply making getting to know more available. It gives a effective device for transforming academic structures and growing new opportunities for students worldwide. By harnessing the entire potential of AI, we can provide personalized, inclusive, and scalable schooling that could meet the diverse needs of newbies across the globe. However, cautious attention should be given to the moral, social, and technological demanding situations that accompany the tremendous adoption of AI in schooling. If these demanding situations are addressed thoughtfully and collaboratively, AI has the ability to revolutionize schooling and make it more on hand to each person, irrespective of their historical past or instances.

5.2. Supporting Students with Disabilities Through AI

Artificial Intelligence (AI) holds substantial promise for transforming the instructional experiences of students with disabilities. By supplying personalized, adaptive learning tools, AI can assist create an inclusive instructional surroundings that comprises the diverse needs of those college students. Through advancements in AI-driven technology, students with bodily, sensory, and cognitive impairments can acquire tailored support, ensuring that education will become extra available, enticing, and effective.

One of the most great blessings of AI in assisting college students with disabilities is its ability to customize studying in actual-time. Traditional lecture room environments might also warfare to cater to the particular wishes of students with disabilities because of time, resource, and instructor-student ratio constraints. AI systems, however, are designed to evaluate person gaining knowledge of patterns, strengths, and challenges, allowing them to provide a custom gaining knowledge of revel in that adapts to every pupil's tempo and capabilities. For example, AI can examine a student's reading comprehension stage and adjust the textual content trouble for this reason, making sure that the pupil is both challenged and supported correctly.

For college students with visible impairments, AI technologies such as text-to-speech structures can examine aloud digital content material, making it on hand without requiring bodily interaction. These systems can convert printed text into auditory form, allowing visually impaired college students to get entry to books, articles, and academic substances that might otherwise be unavailable to them. Furthermore, AI-powered photo reputation tools can describe pictures and diagrams, which would be mainly beneficial for topics which include arithmetic or science, wherein visual aids play a critical position in understanding ideas.

In addition to text-to-speech technologies, AI-based totally speech-to-text structures also are crucial gear for students with listening to impairments. These structures convert spoken phrases into written textual content in actual-time, making lectures, discussions, and study room activities greater reachable to college students who are deaf or difficult of hearing. AI can also help students in language getting to know by means of supplying actual-time captions, signal language translation, or even creating visible cues that help students understand complicated ideas while not having to depend on conventional verbal verbal exchange.

Another location wherein AI can drastically impact college students with disabilities is in growing adaptive learning environments that cater to students with cognitive disabilities. AI can examine a student's development and offer centered interventions whilst vital, helping college students with conditions consisting of dyslexia, ADHD, or autism spectrum issues. For example, AI-powered gaining knowledge of platforms can wreck down complicated responsibilities into smaller, more conceivable steps, allowing college students to technique demanding situations gradually and at their very own pace. Additionally, AI-driven academic equipment can display the scholar's engagement degree and regulate content material or teaching strategies based at the student's consciousness, offering support to those who may additionally battle with attention or concentration issues.

Furthermore, AI can help college students with mobility impairments by means of allowing extra bendy learning environments. AI systems may be included with digital school rooms, supplying college students the potential to engage in training, participate in institution discussions, and access learning materials from home or different non-traditional settings. This is specifically crucial for students who cannot attend faculty because of physical barriers, as AI permits them to have interaction with their friends and instructors remotely whilst nevertheless receiving a first rate training.

AI technologies additionally have the ability to enhance social and emotional support for students with disabilities. By using AI-based totally equipment, educators can better understand the emotional states of students and regulate their coaching strategies as a consequence. AI can analyze facial expressions, tone of voice, or even physiological information to assess how a pupil is feeling and whether they're struggling with emotional or behavioral challenges. This records can then help educators provide additional support or accommodations to ensure that students with disabilities sense emotionally supported in the classroom.

However, whilst the blessings of AI in supporting college students with disabilities are tremendous, there also are ability challenges and ethical issues. One problem is the hazard of over-reliance on AI structures, which can inadvertently update the position of human educators in presenting emotional and social help. It is critical that AI is seen as a complementary tool as opposed to an alternative choice to human interaction. Teachers and academic team of workers should continue to be at the forefront of helping college students' emotional and social improvement, with AI serving as a tool that complements, rather than diminishes, human connection.

Additionally, the use of AI in training increases questions about facts privateness and safety. Since AI systems often collect big amounts of personal information about students, together with their studying styles, behavioral tendencies, and likely even fitness statistics, it's far crucial that sturdy safeguards are in area to shield this touchy records. Educational establishments should make sure that AI equipment observe data protection rules and that scholars' privacy is respected. Furthermore, AI builders have to be obvious about how statistics is accumulated, used, and saved, and dad and mom and students should be knowledgeable about the potential risks and advantages of using AI technologies.

Finally, even as AI can appreciably improve get right of entry to to training for students with disabilities, it is important to consider the accessibility of the technology itself. AI equipment must be designed with inclusivity in thoughts, making sure that they may be used by college students with varying types of disabilities. This calls for collaboration among AI builders, educators, and disability advocates to make certain that AI systems aren't handiest effective but additionally genuinely reachable to all students, no matter their disabilities.

In conclusion, AI has the ability to revolutionize the manner we support college students with disabilities, making schooling extra handy, customized, and inclusive. By making use of AI technology, educators can offer tailor-made mastering reviews, help college students with a number of impairments, and create a more inclusive instructional surroundings for all. However, as with all technological advancement, it's miles important that AI in schooling is applied thoughtfully, with cautious attention to ethical considerations, data privacy, and inclusivity. When used responsibly, AI can substantially enhance the educational experiences and opportunities for college students with disabilities, supporting them attain their full capability.

5.3. Digital Education and Global Access

Digital training has emerged as one of the maximum transformative forces in present day schooling, reshaping how learning is brought and experienced round the sector. With the fast enlargement of internet get admission to and technological advancements, digital platforms and online gaining knowledge of tools are now attaining a broader global target market, making training extra reachable to human beings from various backgrounds and areas.

One of the primary advantages of virtual schooling is its capacity to conquer geographical and logistical boundaries. In many parts of the sector, particularly in rural and faraway regions, get right of entry to to standard academic establishments can be restrained because of factors inclusive of lack of infrastructure, scarcity of qualified instructors, or economic constraints. Digital schooling can bridge this gap by way of allowing college students to access gaining knowledge of substances, attend digital instructions, and have interaction with instructors from everywhere with an internet connection. This democratization of schooling allows college students to receive fantastic preparation regardless of their region, supplying possibilities for lifelong getting to know and skill improvement.

For example, big open online courses (MOOCs) presented through prestigious universities which includes Harvard, MIT, and Stanford are now available to every person with an internet connection. These courses cowl a extensive range of topics, from laptop science to commercial enterprise, arts, and arts, offering freshmen the danger to get entry to international-elegance education with out the want to bodily attend a college. Similarly, digital structures like Coursera, edX, and Khan Academy provide novices with unfastened or low-value guides, in addition expanding get admission to to educational assets that might otherwise be out of reach for many people.

In addition to MOOCs, virtual training tools also encompass eBooks, video lectures, interactive simulations, and online checks, all of which may be tailored to individual gaining knowledge of patterns and wishes. These resources allow college students to analyze at their personal tempo, revisit concepts as wished, and get admission to guide thru on line forums or peer networks. For beginners in underdeveloped or battle-affected regions, digital schooling can offer an alternative to traditional training, where academic centers may be unavailable or hazardous.

Furthermore, digital training has the capability to offer specialised gaining knowledge of opportunities for marginalized businesses, including women, refugees, and those with disabilities. In many parts of the world, cultural or social boundaries may additionally limit access to schooling for these corporations. Digital platforms, however, can provide a safe and available area for people to learn and develop abilities, assisting them conquer those limitations. For instance, digital schooling projects such as those aimed toward teaching girls in developing countries offer an opportunity to traditional schooling, empowering women to pursue their schooling and improve their destiny potentialities.

However, in spite of the capability of digital training to sell international get admission to, considerable challenges remain in making sure that those opportunities are truely inclusive. One of the primary obstacles is the virtual divide – the gap among those who've get admission to to the net and the important technology and those who do not. In many low-profits countries or rural areas, net access is limited or non-existent, or even where it is available, the infrastructure may be insufficient to aid tremendous virtual schooling. This disparity in get entry to to technology can create a -tiered schooling system, wherein college students in greater evolved areas have get admission to to superior learning gear and resources, whilst those in less developed areas are left at the back of.

Moreover, the value of gadgets, internet connectivity, and digital mastering systems can be prohibitive for plenty households and communities. While some governments and agencies are working to address these issues with the aid of offering subsidized internet get right of entry to or donating devices, the space remains extensive in many areas. As a result, students from low-profits backgrounds or rural regions may also warfare to take full gain of digital schooling possibilities, exacerbating current inequalities in education get entry to.

In addition to the demanding situations of infrastructure and affordability, digital education additionally raises concerns about the quality of getting to know. While digital structures provide get entry to to a wealth of information, the satisfactory of that statistics can range significantly. In a few instances, digital assets may also lack the intensity or rigor of traditional school room guidance, and college students may additionally war to have interaction with content that isn't always nicely-designed or interactive. Furthermore, the absence of in-individual training can restrict opportunities for college kids to interact in discussions, ask questions, or acquire immediate feedback from instructors, which are important components of the gaining knowledge of system.

To address those demanding situations, it is crucial that virtual schooling is included into broader educational systems in methods that supplement and enhance traditional kinds of mastering. This method ensuring that digital equipment are used along with face-to-face guidance, with teachers presenting steering and help to students as they navigate on line mastering environments. Additionally, the best of virtual instructional content have to be a top precedence, with platforms and institutions making sure that assets are nicely-curated, updated, and designed to promote significant engagement and critical questioning.

Governments, NGOs, and international corporations also have a role to play in promoting international get admission to to virtual training. By making an investment in virtual infrastructure, offering funding for net get entry to, and helping projects that concentrate on bridging the virtual divide, those organizations can help create a more equitable global education machine. For instance, the United Nations' Sustainable Development Goals (SDGs) include a focal point on ensuring inclusive and equitable great education and selling lifelong getting to know opportunities for all, which aligns with the objectives of expanding virtual training get right of entry to.

In addition to enhancing infrastructure, policymakers must additionally consider the cultural, linguistic, and pedagogical diversity of newbies when designing virtual training tasks. For example, on-line courses should be to be had in more than one languages, with content material adapted to the unique cultural contexts and studying alternatives of different areas. Moreover, virtual platforms should offer functions that help college students with disabilities, ensuring that each one beginners have identical get admission to to educational sources.

The role of teachers and educators within the digital education landscape is also crucial. Teachers need to be ready with the competencies and information necessary to efficiently combine virtual tools into their teaching practices. This requires ongoing expert development and aid to help educators navigate the complexities of digital training and make sure that they are able to provide meaningful studying stories for their students. Furthermore, virtual schooling need to no longer replace the teacher-student courting, which stays a crucial component of effective studying. Instead, technology should be used to decorate this relationship through imparting tools that permit teachers to better recognize their college students' needs and tailor guidance as a consequence.

In end, virtual education gives tremendous potential to extend get right of entry to to exceptional education globally, helping to triumph over geographical, financial, and social boundaries. By leveraging virtual platforms, rookies from all corners of the world can get admission to academic sources, engage with teachers, and pursue their instructional dreams. However, for virtual education to reach its complete potential, it is crucial that governments, agencies, and educators work together to address the challenges of the digital divide, ensure the best of on line mastering content, and create inclusive, equitable systems that offer opportunities for all college students, regardless of their background or place. Through those efforts, virtual training can assist transform the educational panorama and provide a extra available and equitable destiny for newbies around the world.

5.4. Creating Inclusive Learning Environments with AI

Creating absolutely inclusive gaining knowledge of environments has lengthy been a foundational aim of tutorial theory and practice. Such environments apprehend and celebrate range amongst newcomers, presenting equitable opportunities for all students to have interaction, be successful, and thrive irrespective of their backgrounds, skills, or identities. With the appearance of Artificial Intelligence (AI), new equipment and methodologies have emerged that considerably beautify the ability of educators and establishments to layout, put in force, and sustain inclusivity in education. AI's potential to customize studying, detect obstacles, and aid various wishes offers transformative capability to dismantle conventional limitations and foster environments where each learner can participate absolutely and meaningfully.

At its core, inclusivity in education calls for recognizing the multiplicity of learner differences—cognitive styles, cultural backgrounds, linguistic abilities, bodily and sensory disabilities, socio-economic factors, and emotional needs. Historically, instructional systems often relied on one-length-suits-all processes that failed to accommodate such range, resulting in exclusion or marginalization of many students. AI technologies, via evaluation, allow granular customization and responsiveness that may adapt to each learner's particular profile, thereby increasing the definition and attain of inclusion.

One giant way AI contributes to inclusivity is through personalized gaining knowledge of pathways. Adaptive studying platforms analyze character rookies' strengths, weaknesses, and preferences, dynamically editing content trouble, layout, and pacing to healthy their desires. For students with learning disabilities such as dyslexia, attention deficit hyperactivity disease (ADHD), or autism spectrum disease, AI systems can offer tailored helps—like textual content-to-speech, visual aids, simplified instructions, or interactive simulations—that make content material greater reachable and tasty. These individualized techniques lessen frustration and barriers, empowering students who might otherwise battle in standardized settings.

Moreover, AI-driven assistive technology provide direct guide to newbies with bodily, sensory, or cognitive impairments. For instance, speech reputation and herbal language processing enable voice instructions and dictation for college kids with motor demanding situations. Real-time captioning and signal language avatars beautify communique for those with hearing impairments. Eye-monitoring and mind-laptop interface technology open possibilities for college kids with severe mobility obstacles to engage with virtual content. By integrating such assistive tools inside mainstream gaining knowledge of systems, AI allows normalize accessibility and bridges gaps that traditional lodges might overlook or inadequately cope with.

Language range additionally advantages substantially from AI-enabled inclusivity. Multilingual novices often face hurdles when coaching is introduced solely in a dominant language. AI-powered translation, transcription, and language gaining knowledge of equipment can provide instant linguistic aid, permitting college students to get right of entry to content material in their native language or exercise language acquisition at personalized paces. Furthermore, AI can perceive culturally applicable content and adapt examples or contexts to resonate with numerous backgrounds, fostering a extra welcoming and relatable instructional revel in.

Beyond individualized supports, AI facilitates popular layout for getting to know (UDL) principles with the aid of allowing a couple of manner of representation, expression, and engagement. For example, academic substances may be offered in diverse codecs—textual content, audio, video, interactive simulations—giving novices alternatives to have interaction in ways that fit their alternatives or needs. AI algorithms can reveal engagement patterns and propose alternative content material transport techniques if a learner is struggling, for that reason proactively disposing of obstacles to participation.

In study room settings, AI-powered analytics provide educators with actionable insights approximately the inclusivity of their coaching practices. By studying participation prices, venture final touch, and evaluation effects across unique pupil corporations, AI can highlight disparities which could suggest systemic exclusion or bias. Teachers can then interfere with targeted strategies, along with differentiated education or peer assist initiatives. Additionally, AI can assist inclusive study room management through tracking social dynamics, detecting bullying or marginalization, and alerting educators to interfere early.

The design and deployment of AI itself have to adhere to inclusivity concepts. Inclusive AI development involves various datasets, participatory layout with stakeholders from underrepresented organizations, and non-stop bias auditing. Failure to accomplish that dangers replicating or amplifying societal inequities thru educational technologies. For instance, AI structures skilled predominantly on facts from majority populations can also misinterpret behaviors or wishes of minority inexperienced persons, main to inaccurate tips or exclusionary outcomes. Inclusive AI improvement is crucial to make certain that the advantages of adaptive gaining knowledge of and accessibility equipment are equitably distributed.

Ethical issues are paramount in fostering inclusive AI-more advantageous gaining knowledge of environments. Transparency about how AI systems make decisions, protections for scholar information privacy, and admire for learner autonomy need to be integrated into all degrees of implementation. Educators and college students should have corporation to override or personalize AI interventions, ensuring that technology helps human judgment as opposed to replacing it. Building agree with in AI's function within inclusive training requires open verbal exchange and ongoing dialogue amongst all stakeholders.

Furthermore, AI gives opportunities to beautify social-emotional mastering (SEL) and promote inclusivity beyond instructional fulfillment. Intelligent systems can become aware of symptoms of emotional distress, social isolation, or anxiety, especially in susceptible students. By alerting educators or suggesting supportive assets, AI contributes to developing nurturing environments where each learner feels valued and supported. Inclusive education accordingly extends into holistic improvement, encompassing properly-being as well as highbrow increase.

Looking ahead, the combination of AI with rising technology which includes virtual and augmented truth promises even greater immersive and inclusive educational studies. Imagine students with mobility demanding situations exploring digital field trips, or language freshmen conducting culturally wealthy, simulated conversations that adapt to their talent level. These technologies, powered by way of AI, will further destroy down bodily, social, and cognitive boundaries, starting get entry to to experiential gaining knowledge of previously unattainable for lots.

AI has the capability to revolutionize the creation of inclusive learning environments with the aid of allowing personalization, accessibility, cultural responsiveness, and social-emotional assist at extraordinary scales. However, knowing this capacity calls for intentional design, moral dedication, and collaborative engagement among educators, technologists, policymakers, and learners themselves. When inclusivity is embedded at the heart of AI-superior training, it transforms not only person lives however additionally the cloth of society, fostering fairness, dignity, and possibility for all.

5.5. AI-Powered Tools for Diverse Learning Styles

Every learner approaches schooling with a unique set of alternatives, strengths, and cognitive styles—normally referred to as learning patterns. These styles may include visual, auditory, kinesthetic, reading/writing choices, or combinations thereof. Recognizing and accommodating this variety is crucial to maximizing engagement, comprehension, and retention. Artificial Intelligence (AI) offers effective gear to identify, adapt to, and assist diverse mastering patterns at an character level, remodeling schooling from a one-length-fits-all version into a in reality personalised revel in.

Traditionally, educators have confronted challenges in tailoring education to numerous studying styles because of constraints in time, resources, and sophistication sizes. AI-powered systems, however, can constantly collect and analyze data on learner interactions—such as how college students respond to exclusive content formats, how speedy they draw close concepts offered in diverse modalities, and their performance throughout multimedia obligations. By interpreting this facts, AI algorithms broaden dynamic learner profiles that mirror now not handiest preferred patterns but also contextual elements including temper, motivation, and cognitive load.

One key utility of AI is in adaptive content material delivery, wherein materials are custom designed to in shape character learning possibilities. For example, a scholar with a visual learning fashion would possibly acquire infographics, films, and animations, at the same time as an auditory learner can be supplied podcasts, narrated explanations, or voice-primarily based quizzes. Kinesthetic beginners advantage from interactive simulations and palms-on virtual labs powered via AI that modify complexity based on real-time comments. By delivering content in the learner's favored modes, AI enhances engagement and enables deeper understanding.

Natural Language Processing (NLP) and speech popularity technology further expand the reach of AI to support auditory and verbal getting to know styles. Intelligent tutoring systems prepared with conversational marketers or chatbots engage newcomers in speak, asking questions, providing causes, and imparting clarifications in a manner corresponding to human tutors. These systems can come across whilst a student struggles to comprehend a idea and switch modalities—possibly from text to voice—to higher fit the learner's desires.

AI also excels in multimodal mastering environments, which combine multiple sensory inputs to cater to complex and evolving mastering choices. Through sensor information, eye tracking, and interaction logs, AI video display units learner engagement and adjusts academic techniques for this reason. For instance, if a learner indicates symptoms of fatigue at some stage in a prolonged video, the gadget might introduce an interactive exercising or transfer to textual content to maintain attention. This fluid model helps beginners whose patterns fluctuate based on context, content material complexity, or emotional country.

Moreover, AI-driven studying analytics offer educators with insights into the variety of mastering patterns within their classrooms. Dashboards and reports summarize which modalities resonate with particular college students or businesses, allowing instructors to design mixed lessons that deal with varied needs. This data-driven technique fosters differentiated practise with out overwhelming educators, bridging the distance between individualization and scalability.

AI also supports metacognitive development by using supporting newcomers turn out to be privy to their very own learning styles and strategies. Personalized comments and reflective activates generated by AI encourage college students to test with distinct modalities and discover what works satisfactory for them. Over time, novices construct self-law abilities, adapting their processes to optimize effects throughout topics and contexts.

The integration of AI with rising technologies like virtual fact (VR) and augmented truth (AR) opens in addition possibilities for catering to diverse gaining knowledge of styles. Immersive environments can simulate actual-international scenarios for kinesthetic rookies, provide rich visual contexts, and incorporate spatial audio cues. AI algorithms within those environments modify stories based on learner responses, ensuring alignment with individual alternatives and wishes.

In addition to instructional content, AI-powered gear facilitate social and emotional gaining knowledge of (SEL) tailored to numerous communique and interaction patterns. Systems can understand whilst learners select collaborative organization work, person mirrored image, or interactive storytelling, adapting social dynamics and sports to optimize engagement and emotional well-being.

However, the a success deployment of AI tools for numerous getting to know patterns calls for cautious interest to ethical and accessibility concerns. Algorithms ought to learn on inclusive datasets to keep away from reinforcing biases that could marginalize certain learner companies. Transparency approximately records series and utilization fosters agree with among newbies and educators. Importantly, AI have to empower human educators as opposed to replace them, serving as an augmentative era that enhances pedagogical choice-making.

Furthermore, AI systems need to stay bendy and keep away from rigidly categorizing freshmen, recognizing that people may additionally showcase multiple studying patterns or shift alternatives depending on content material and context. Overemphasis on fixed patterns risks pigeonholing students and restricting exposure to alternative techniques that foster cognitive growth.

AI-powered equipment offer extraordinary opportunities to guide and have a good time the range of gaining knowledge of styles inside academic environments. By constantly adapting content transport, offering multimodal reports, and empowering metacognitive focus, AI transforms mastering into a customized, engaging, and effective journey. When combined with thoughtful human guidance and ethical implementation, those technologies keep the promise of unlocking every learner's capacity and fostering a greater inclusive and dynamic educational panorama.

CHAPTER 6

AI and the Revolution in Education

6.1. Future Trends in Education

Education has usually been an evolving subject, continuously present process adjustments during history. With the advancement of era, those changes have turn out to be quicker and more profound. Artificial intelligence (AI) is one of the maximum extensive driving forces in the back of this evolution, with the capability to revolutionize educational systems. In the future, tendencies in schooling will now not most effective rework students' reviews but also make getting to know approaches more efficient and interactive.

The position of AI in training goes a long way beyond the digitization of coaching materials and offering customized content to college students. AI will decide the route of instructional trends, reshape teaching methods, and profoundly adjust the way academic establishments perform.

One of the most critical trends in training is the shift in the direction of presenting customized learning experiences that cater to the individual needs of college students. Every scholar learns in another way, with various speeds, styles, and necessities. AI can deal with those differences by using supplying each pupil with the maximum appropriate content, materials, and coaching methods.

AI will analyze students' preceding performances, studying styles, strengths, and weaknesses to create personalized mastering plans. In the future, AI-powered structures will continuously music college students' progress, suggesting the maximum suitable learning pathways for them. This personalised technique lets in students to research at their own pace, that can drastically enhance universal academic performance.

The destiny of AI in education may also be built upon mastering analytics. Learning analytics includes accumulating and analyzing student facts to provide significant insights into their studying processes. AI will work with massive volumes of statistics, allowing the evaluation of scholar performance with unheard of precision. Teachers and educational establishments might be able to higher apprehend college students' gaining knowledge of journeys, which lets in for extra targeted interventions.

AI will continuously track statistics on pupil participation, take a look at effects, interactions, and different overall performance metrics. With this information, instructors can identify areas where college students are struggling and provide guidance consequently. Additionally, AI structures can expect capability disasters and ship early warnings to instructors, allowing them to interfere on the proper time. As mastering analytics maintain to conform, instructional strategies are anticipated to emerge as even extra personalised and effective.

Another sizable trend within the future of schooling is the multiplied adoption of hybrid mastering models. Hybrid learning combines conventional face-to-face training with online gaining knowledge of. AI will play a critical function in making these structures a hit. AI can provide interactive gaining knowledge of substances for students in on-line environments while also enhancing in-magnificence interactions between instructors and students.

AI-supported hybrid getting to know systems will permit college students to simultaneously have interaction in bodily school rooms and online platforms, supplying extra flexibility and customized getting to know reports. Students could be able to examine at their own pace, while instructors can tune their progress extra carefully. This version will empower each college students and educators, making schooling extra dynamic and adaptable.

In the future, the function of teachers may shift. While AI can facilitate and streamline the teaching technique, it's going to not replace instructors altogether. AI will assist instructors in guiding, mentoring, and offering emotional intelligence, that are vital components of teaching. AI could make lecture room management greater efficient, but the human connection between teachers and college students will continue to be essential.

AI-powered academic systems will deliver instructors greater freedom and versatility, allowing them to adopt greater innovative and pupil-focused teaching methods. Teachers can be capable of make extra knowledgeable choices primarily based at the information furnished by way of AI structures, focusing on students' strengths and regions that require attention.

One of the vital tendencies for the future is the growth in accessibility in schooling. AI has the capacity to reduce academic inequalities. AI-pushed solutions can considerably enhance access to schooling for college kids in developing areas and for people with disabilities. AI-primarily based tools can cater to the one-of-a-kind wishes of students and integrate them into more inclusive studying environments.

AI can create customized learning substances for college kids with disabilities, consisting of people with visual or listening to impairments, or the ones who've getting to know problems. This creates a greater inclusive schooling machine, permitting all college students to examine at their own pace and in a way that suits their wishes. AI can bridge gaps in educational opportunities and offer a fairer getting to know revel in for college students from all backgrounds.

The development of generation is making training greater handy on a international scale. AI will play a crucial function in growing worldwide get right of entry to to schooling. With online learning systems and AI-supported equipment, students from all over the international can get entry to academic resources. AI can wreck down language obstacles, provide learning materials in college students' native languages, and customise content to decorate the getting to know experience.

These traits will offer academic possibilities, specifically for students in faraway areas and developing nations, thereby addressing global educational disparities. AI will no longer simplest provide getting to know substances however additionally provide gear to make education greater interactive and on hand, permitting students to obtain a better high-quality of training regardless of their area.

One of the important thing traits may be the emergence of completely new instructional fashions. AI will enable the development of revolutionary mastering methods that make the getting to know method more efficient, interactive, and personalized. These new fashions will go past the content material of education and reshape the roles of college students, teachers, and academic establishments.

AI can provide college students with continuous remarks, song their learning velocity, and offer private steerage. Educational systems that include these new fashions can be more powerful, permitting students to research better and quicker. Teachers may even advantage from more accurate insights into students' desires and skills, if you want to enhance ordinary instructional effects.

6.2. The New Educational Model: AI and Educational Institutions

The rise of synthetic intelligence (AI) isn't always most effective transforming how students research but is likewise reshaping the fundamental structures of instructional institutions. In the destiny, academic establishments could be deeply intertwined with AI technology, leading to a complete rethinking of conventional academic models. AI will introduce new methodologies, gear, and tactics, redefining the manner training is added, accessed, and experienced.

One of the number one changes AI will bring to instructional establishments is the introduction of AI-powered management systems. These structures will streamline administrative duties, improve operational efficiency, and optimize aid allocation. AI can automate numerous administrative features such as grading, scheduling, attendance, and evaluation tracking, permitting educators and administrators to cognizance on greater meaningful duties like student engagement and curriculum development.

These AI control systems may even offer treasured statistics analytics, supporting schools and universities make data-pushed choices. For example, AI can analyze student performance and engagement statistics to perceive tendencies, forecast future results, and endorse interventions to improve ordinary performance. This predictive capability will permit academic institutions to proactively cope with troubles earlier than they amplify, ensuring that scholars receive the assist they need to be successful.

AI can even assist educational institutions flow closer to customized learning pathways, wherein each student's individual needs, hobbies, and mastering styles are taken into account. With AI, institutions can be able to create customized academic studies for college kids, ensuring that they are getting to know at their own tempo and in ways that match them exceptional. AI will enable educators to supply greater focused instruction, ensuring that no scholar is left at the back of.

AI can examine student statistics, inclusive of past educational performance, gaining knowledge of possibilities, and regions of war, to create personalised gaining knowledge of plans. These plans can adapt in actual-time based totally on a student's progress, presenting additional resources or adjusting the problem level of materials as needed. This tailor-made method no longer only enhances pupil engagement but also ensures that students reach their complete capacity through supplying them with the proper aid at the proper time.

In addition to transforming administrative functions, AI will revolutionize teaching methods. AI will aid instructors with the aid of presenting them a big range of coaching equipment that decorate scholar engagement and enhance studying consequences. AI-driven equipment including shrewd tutoring structures, virtual lecture rooms, and interactive getting to know systems will help create a greater attractive, dynamic, and responsive gaining knowledge of surroundings.

For instance, AI-powered tutoring structures can provide students with immediately comments and reasons, allowing them to paintings at their very own pace and obtain individualized interest out of doors of conventional school room hours. These systems can simulate human-like interactions, supplying college students with explanations, examples, and steering as wanted. By integrating AI into school room teaching, educators can be able to use statistics-pushed insights to tailor their training and adapt to college students' particular studying wishes.

The traditional classroom setup is likewise set to adapt inside the age of AI. Educational institutions will an increasing number of adopt sensible learning systems and virtual classrooms that provide greater flexible and interactive getting to know studies. These platforms can integrate AI technology consisting of natural language processing, system gaining knowledge of, and adaptive learning algorithms to create customized studying studies for each student.

Digital classrooms will permit students to interact with content material through diverse multimedia codecs, which include video, simulations, and virtual reality (VR). These technologies, supported through AI, will offer immersive mastering stories that go past the restrictions of traditional textbooks and static training. Students may have get right of entry to to a much broader range of assets and mastering substances, and they'll be able to engage in greater hands-on and experiential getting to know.

AI will also facilitate actual-time collaboration in digital lecture rooms, permitting students to paintings collectively across geographical obstacles. AI equipment can tune scholar interactions, analyze institution dynamics, and advocate collaborative activities based totally on college students' strengths and weaknesses, fostering a more interactive and attractive gaining knowledge of environment.

Educational establishments global will advantage from AI's potential to bridge geographical and cultural divides. AI will facilitate global collaboration with the aid of imparting students with get admission to to a diverse range of studying substances and assets from distinctive components of the sector. Institutions can use AI-pushed gear to overcome language boundaries, translate substances, and make certain that scholars have get entry to to instructional content in their local languages.

AI's ability to offer customized studying experiences could be specifically useful for students in underserved regions or people with restrained access to conventional instructional assets. By making academic content material greater reachable, AI will help lessen instructional inequalities, imparting all college students with same possibilities for studying and boom.

Furthermore, AI can allow international partnerships between academic establishments, encouraging the sharing of information, studies, and resources. This worldwide network of AI-more advantageous education structures will foster pass-cultural understanding and collaboration, preparing students for the interconnected international they will paintings in.

As AI becomes an quintessential part of academic institutions, there are important moral issues that ought to be addressed. One of the number one issues is the privacy and security of pupil facts. AI systems depend heavily on records to customise learning reports and tune pupil performance. Educational institutions will need to make certain that scholar information is saved securely and that privateness is respected.

Another key trouble is the capability for AI to exacerbate present inequalities in schooling. While AI has the ability to make education extra inclusive, it may additionally deepen the digital divide if not implemented equitably. Educational institutions must ensure that every one students have get right of entry to to the necessary generation and sources to advantage from AI-improved mastering.

Additionally, as AI takes on greater decision-making roles in education, there may be a situation that it may update human instructors or decrease the personalized touch in education. Educational institutions will need to strike a stability among leveraging AI to enhance learning results and maintaining the human element that is critical to education. Teachers will keep to play a critical position in fostering creativity, vital wondering, and emotional intelligence in students, areas wherein AI can't completely replace human input.

Looking beforehand, instructional establishments might be converted through AI, ensuing in a more dynamic, customized, and on hand getting to know environment. As AI continues to conform, educational structures will want to evolve to make sure that scholars receive the high-quality possible schooling even as additionally addressing moral concerns and making sure equitable get admission to to technology.

AI will enable academic establishments to offer more personalised, flexible, and green getting to know stories for students, in the long run leading to better mastering outcomes. The destiny of education will be one where technology and human understanding work together to create a more inclusive, effective, and progressive mastering environment for all college students.

As AI maintains to reshape education, the destiny of educational institutions looks promising, presenting new possibilities for students and educators alike. The integration of AI will foster a greater adaptive and green education device, paving the manner for a future where mastering is tailored to every pupil's unique needs and abilities, and academic institutions remain at the leading edge of innovation.

6.3. Learning Analytics and Artificial Intelligence

Learning analytics, blended with artificial intelligence (AI), represents a innovative shift in the area of schooling, bringing information-pushed insights to the leading edge of coaching and learning methods. This intersection of AI and mastering analytics isn't always merely a trend however a essential transformation to be able to form the future of educational structures, making them greater personalised, efficient, and conscious of character learning desires. Through the electricity of AI, studying analytics can liberate new capacity in understanding scholar conduct, enhancing academic consequences, and optimizing coaching methods.

Learning analytics refers to the collection, size, and evaluation of statistics regarding novices and their contexts to improve learning and coaching. This statistics can come from numerous sources, including pupil assessments, participation in digital structures, interplay with gaining knowledge of assets, and even social media or verbal exchange gear used inside the classroom. By systematically gathering and studying this information, educators can benefit deeper insights into student development, discover getting to know patterns, and make informed choices to enhance the learning revel in.

Traditionally, mastering analytics has targeted on retrospective evaluation, in which information from past activities is used to assess student overall performance.

However, with the incorporation of AI technologies, learning analytics can now function in real-time, supplying up-to-date insights that assist educators and institutions adapt swiftly to rising challenges.

AI's role in mastering analytics is to process and examine massive volumes of records at a speed and scale that could be impossible for humans to reap. AI algorithms, in particular the ones in the domains of system learning and deep getting to know, can become aware of complex patterns in the statistics that human educators may neglect. By leveraging these patterns, AI could make predictions about scholar overall performance, engagement, and ability risks, taking into consideration early intervention and personalised support.

AI-driven studying analytics tools can continuously display a student's development, presenting remarks on regions wherein they'll be struggling or excelling. These gear can expect gaining knowledge of effects, along with the chance of success in a course, and offer recommendations for interventions that might enhance a scholar's overall performance. This predictive functionality not best helps college students however also presents precious records for teachers to refine their teaching strategies and strategies.

AI also can help find hidden elements that influence learning results, inclusive of emotional states, motivation degrees, and social interactions, which can be difficult to measure thru traditional assessment strategies. By reading behavioral records, AI can provide a more complete knowledge of the getting to know technique, allowing educators to cater to the various wishes of their students.

One of the maximum powerful aspects of AI and gaining knowledge of analytics is the potential to offer actual-time insights into student mastering. This permits for a customised learning enjoy, wherein coaching and sources may be tailored to the individual desires of every pupil. With AI, mastering analytics can track a student's progress throughout multiple dimensions, along with comprehension, participation, and engagement, adjusting the mastering pathway based totally on real-time data.

For example, AI can detect whilst a pupil is suffering with a selected concept and robotically propose extra resources, exercise sporting events, or alternative reasons. Similarly, if a pupil is excelling, the system can offer superior materials to project them in addition. By turning in content material this is precisely aligned with the learner's cutting-edge level of expertise, AI permits an adaptive gaining knowledge of surroundings that maximizes every student's ability.

Moreover, real-time analytics permits for immediate feedback, making sure that students are not left looking forward to evaluation outcomes. This timely remarks loop no longer only allows college students stay heading in the right direction however additionally fosters a greater attractive and motivating mastering experience.

One of the best benefits of AI-pushed mastering analytics is the capability to are expecting scholar performance and effects. By analyzing historical statistics and styles of scholar conduct, AI can forecast ability challenges a pupil might face and recommend early interventions to prevent failure. For instance, AI can perceive college students who're liable to dropping out or failing a course based totally on factors together with engagement tiers, completion fees of assignments, and take a look at overall performance.

Educators and administrators can use these predictions to enforce focused interventions, consisting of additional tutoring, mentoring, or modifications in academic techniques. Early intervention allows for well timed guide, making sure that students do no longer fall too a long way at the back of and increasing the chances of successful consequences. This proactive method to student aid can significantly reduce dropout charges and enhance typical academic performance.

In addition, predictive analytics can be used to identify broader developments and styles inside instructional systems. For example, AI can analyze performance facts throughout numerous guides and demographics to discover institutional-wide issues, which includes gaps in scholar fulfillment or disparities in effects amongst extraordinary student organizations. These insights can guide institutional reforms, making sure that every one students have the possibility to prevail.

AI-powered gaining knowledge of analytics not only benefit college students but additionally provide precious insights to educators. Teachers can use statistics to mirror on their teaching techniques, become aware of regions in which college students are suffering, and modify their educational strategies hence. For example, if a good sized quantity of college students are having problem know-how a specific concept, a teacher can use analytics to pick out the foundation cause and adjust the lesson plan or coaching technique.

AI also can provide instructors with a deeper understanding of man or woman college students, highlighting their strengths, weaknesses, and getting to know choices. This information permits educators to offer more tailor-made education and allocate sources greater successfully, ensuring that every scholar receives the assist they need to succeed.

Moreover, studying analytics can assist teachers song their own overall performance and expert development. By reading feedback and assessments from college students, AI can spotlight regions wherein a instructor may want extra education or assist. This continuous remarks loop fosters a subculture of development, supporting educators become greater effective of their roles.

Beyond individual college students and teachers, AI-driven learning analytics also offer educational institutions with precious insights into basic performance and institutional effectiveness. Educational leaders can use information to evaluate the success of various applications, courses, and coaching strategies, making informed decisions about where to allocate assets and a way to enhance institutional policies.

For example, mastering analytics can screen which guides or departments are underperforming, making an allowance for targeted upgrades in curriculum design or coaching best. Similarly, institutions can use analytics to reveal the effectiveness of new technologies, interventions, or academic techniques, making sure that their investments are yielding the desired consequences.

AI can also support institutions in evaluating the effectiveness in their admissions methods, student support services, or even economic resource guidelines. By inspecting the records, establishments can refine their strategies to better meet the wishes in their student populations, in the long run improving the general instructional enjoy.

While the capability of AI and gaining knowledge of analytics is considerable, it is important to cope with the moral implications of using such technologies. The collection and evaluation of student facts increase issues about privacy, records safety, and consent. Educational establishments should make sure that facts is gathered and stored securely, adhering to privacy laws and ethical suggestions to guard students' private facts.

Moreover, there is the chance that data-pushed selection-making may want to perpetuate biases or inequities. If AI algorithms are trained on biased records, they may beef up present disparities in training, main to unfair remedy of sure student businesses. It is critical that institutions take steps to ensure that learning analytics systems are obvious, responsible, and loose from bias.

AI-driven analytics ought to also be used responsibly, making sure that the focal point remains on enhancing gaining knowledge of results and helping pupil fulfillment in preference to exploiting facts for business functions or surveillance. Ethical considerations need to manual the improvement and implementation of AI-powered learning analytics, making sure that the benefits of these technology are found out without compromising scholar rights.

The aggregate of AI and learning analytics is transforming the educational panorama by using providing customized, facts-driven insights that enhance each coaching and gaining knowledge of. By imparting real-time feedback, predicting pupil effects, and permitting focused interventions, AI empowers educators and establishments to create greater adaptive, green, and effective learning environments. However, as with any technology, the mixing of AI into education requires cautious attention of ethical issues, privateness troubles, and the ability for bias. With accountable implementation, AI-driven studying analytics can play a essential role in shaping the future of schooling, making it greater personalized, inclusive, and a hit for all rookies.

6.4. Emerging Technologies Shaping Educational Transformation

The panorama of schooling is undergoing a profound transformation driven through the rapid evolution of rising technology. These innovations are not most effective improving conventional teaching and mastering techniques however additionally redefining the very nature of training itself—how expertise is obtained, shared, and carried out. While Artificial Intelligence (AI) remains a cornerstone of this revolution, a constellation of complementary technology is converging to create dynamic, immersive, and particularly personalized instructional reports. Together, these emerging technology are shaping the future of mastering by means of expanding get entry to, fostering engagement, and equipping learners with the talents vital for a hastily changing world.

One of the most impactful technological traits reshaping training is Extended Reality (XR), an umbrella time period encompassing Virtual Reality (VR), Augmented Reality (AR), and Mixed Reality (MR). XR technologies provide immersive environments wherein inexperienced persons can engage with simulated worlds or overlay digital information onto the physical surroundings. In VR, college students can undertake digital field journeys to ancient web sites, explore the anatomy of the human body in 3D, or interact in realistic technology experiments that would in any other case be impossible due to fee or protection constraints. AR, on the other hand, enhances real-international settings with contextual records—inclusive of interactive models projected onto textbooks or real-time language translation all through conversations. Mixed Reality blends each, allowing seamless interplay among physical and digital items.

The pedagogical blessings of XR lie in its potential to provide experiential learning that caters to numerous learning patterns, promotes energetic engagement, and helps spatial and kinesthetic expertise. As hardware turns into extra less costly and software more state-of-the-art, XR is poised to become a mainstream instructional device, extending possibilities for palms-on getting to know beyond conventional school rooms.

Artificial Intelligence and Machine Learning hold to adapt rapidly, offering the backbone for adaptive learning systems that tailor content material, pacing, and assessment to individual newbies' needs. Beyond personalization, AI enables learning analytics that offer educators insights into student performance, engagement styles, and ability mastering gaps. These analytics guide data-pushed interventions and curriculum changes, fostering more powerful and responsive teaching. Furthermore, advances in Natural Language Processing (NLP) facilitate shrewd tutoring systems and conversational marketers that have interaction with college students in natural language, answering questions, offering reasons, and selling essential questioning.

Another emerging era with transformative capability is Blockchain, typically diagnosed for its position in steady economic transactions. In training, blockchain can revolutionize credentialing and report-preserving through creating immutable, verifiable digital diplomas and transcripts. This complements portability and trustworthiness of academic statistics, facilitating lifelong learning and career mobility. Additionally, blockchain supports decentralized mastering structures, where learners have greater control over their statistics and educational pathways, difficult conventional centralized institutions.

The Internet of Things (IoT) is also shaping educational environments by using connecting physical objects—such as clever whiteboards, wearable gadgets, and environmental sensors—to digital networks. IoT enables real-time tracking of classroom conditions, pupil engagement through biometric feedback, and seamless integration of bodily and digital learning tools. For instance, wearables can tune interest or stress levels, prompting timely interventions or personalized guide. IoT infrastructures contribute to developing smart lecture rooms that are adaptive, green, and learner-targeted.

5G and superior connectivity technology underpin lots of these innovations with the aid of presenting the high-speed, low-latency networks essential for statistics-intensive packages consisting of streaming VR content material or assisting massive-scale AI computations. Enhanced connectivity additionally promotes far flung and hybrid getting to know fashions, breaking geographical boundaries and expanding academic get admission to to underserved areas.

Cloud computing helps scalable and cost-powerful garage and processing of instructional statistics and applications. Cloud systems permit collaborative tools, virtual laboratories, and international school rooms where freshmen and educators from diverse backgrounds interact seamlessly. The democratization of access to powerful computational resources thru the cloud speeds up innovation and inclusion.

Additionally, robotics and embodied AI are beginning to find their vicinity in training. Social robots can function tutors, classroom assistants, or companions, specially in early early life education or unique education contexts. These robots can engage freshmen through interactive dialogues, bodily sports, and emotional assist, contributing to personalized and socially enriched gaining knowledge of studies.

Finally, the integration of massive facts and predictive analytics empowers educational institutions to anticipate developments which includes dropout dangers, route demand, and personnel alignment. By reading great datasets, faculties can optimize useful resource allocation, curriculum layout, and coverage choices to higher serve their communities.

Despite the promise of those rising technologies, challenges stay. Issues along with virtual fairness, privateness, ethical use of information, and the want for educator education should be addressed to ensure that technological transformation translates into meaningful instructional results. Furthermore, technological equipment should be designed with inclusivity and cultural sensitivity at the forefront, keeping off the replication of present biases or obstacles.

Emerging technologies—from XR and AI to blockchain, IoT, and robotics—are together reshaping schooling's panorama in profound methods. They enlarge the boundaries of where, how, and what students examine, fostering environments which can be immersive, personalised, collaborative, and accessible. By thoughtfully integrating those improvements with pedagogical high-quality practices and ethical frameworks, educators and policymakers can harness their transformative ability to build a future of schooling that empowers each learner to thrive in an more and more complicated global.

CHAPTER 7

AI in Education and Economic Impacts

7.1 Economic Implications of AI in Education

Artificial intelligence performs a critical position in enhancing efficiency inside the education quarter. The boom in efficiency is evident in both instructors' and students' capacity to use time and resources more efficaciously, main to reduced prices in academic structures. AI technologies provide computerized systems that lessen instructors' workloads. For instance, time-ingesting obligations together with student checks and reporting can be accomplished speedy and correctly by AI. This lets in instructors greater time to recognition on students immediately.

Moreover, AI structures that tune and analyze pupil overall performance could make the getting to know method more green at every level. Identifying college students' weaknesses and growing customized studying plans allows tailored academic content, increasing standard efficiency. Receiving feedback faster complements college students' mastering experiences, which leads to higher ordinary outcomes within the instructional method.

AI-powered systems drastically reduce the want for human resources, that could lower exertions expenses for educational establishments. For instance, college studunts' participation in AI-supported online publications can minimize the need to boom the variety of instructors. AI, with its huge statistics analytics and learning control structures (LMS), gives scalable answers for instructional institutions at decrease charges.

In addition, AI-driven automated getting to know systems permit college students to progress at their very own tempo. This allows college students to get hold of individualized instruction without teachers needing to devote more time to every student. As a result, academic establishments can reduce standard costs at the same time as offering satisfactory training at a lower fee.

Another financial implication is the fee financial savings visible from the huge adoption of on line instructional platforms. The shift to digital schooling, particularly post-pandemic, has reduced the dependence on bodily classrooms and brought down schooling-related fees. AI-supported structures provide college students the possibility to study everywhere, every time, getting rid of geographical barriers and lowering instructional expenses.

The widespread use of AI in education additionally requires substantial investments in technology infrastructure. This means that educational structures need huge monetary backing to put into effect AI effectively. Developing AI technology and presenting personalized studying applications requires investments in both software and hardware. Educational establishments ought to stable economic resources and make cautious financial plans to deal with those investments.

AI-based totally schooling gives a chief possibility to bridge educational disparities, especially in growing nations. However, to recognise those opportunities, sizeable investments in technology are necessary. In developed nations, funding in technology-primarily based infrastructure can reduce inequalities in schooling, supplying college students a broader variety of tutorial alternatives and getting ready them for the destiny.

One of the broader monetary effects of AI in education is the transformation of the hard work market. Technological advancements will automate positive jobs at the same time as also creating new task possibilities. The education area may be no exception. For instance, there may be increased demand for specialists professional in AI programming, facts analysis, and machine studying.

Additionally, the position of instructors will evolve. Traditional, lecture-primarily based teaching models will supply manner to greater interactive and personalised teaching techniques. Teachers will examine facts provided through AI structures to increase strategies that enable students to examine extra efficaciously. This shift will trade the professional profiles of educators and create a call for for training professionals with new talent units.

In conclusion, artificial intelligence's financial impact on schooling is bringing approximately a profound transformation in each the training quarter and the financial system as an entire. AI's capacity to create extra efficient, value-effective, and available educational systems also comes with new economic dynamics and workforce demands. Adapting to those modifications is vital for the destiny of both training and society.

7.2 AI-Supported Teaching and the Workforce

AI-supported teaching is rapidly transforming the panorama of schooling, and its impact extends a long way past classrooms. It influences the capabilities that students accumulate and the jobs that instructors and administrators play. As AI becomes greater integrated into training, it without delay shapes the group of workers by way of converting the manner individuals study and work.

AI-pushed educational systems can provide customized gaining knowledge of reviews that permit students to recognition on particular capabilities they want to develop. With AI structures that examine student behavior, gaining knowledge of patterns, and overall performance, educators can better recognize every student's desires and offer them with centered resources. This degree of individualized attention enables college students to expand abilties in specialized regions, consisting of trouble-fixing, records analysis, and essential wondering—talents that are essential for the destiny group of workers.

In flip, AI-supported education structures ensure that scholars are better organized for the demanding situations of the unexpectedly evolving task marketplace. As industries emerge as more depending on technology, the call for for employees with a sturdy foundation in STEM (Science, Technology, Engineering, and Mathematics) fields, together with the potential to work alongside AI technologies, will continue to grow. AI's capacity to facilitate personalised, talent-primarily based learning performs a key function in developing these destiny experts.

While AI offers a wealth of blessings in enhancing student mastering, it additionally increases important questions concerning the function of instructors and their relationship with technology. Rather than changing educators, AI is designed to help them, transforming how they technique teaching and the tasks they perform.

In conventional academic models, teachers are regularly chargeable for delivering lectures, grading assignments, and imparting one-on-one attention to college students. AI can automate lots of those capabilities, which include grading, scheduling, and administrative paintings, which frees up teachers' time to consciousness greater on the human elements of schooling, such as mentoring and supplying emotional guide.

This shift lets in educators to use their knowledge in new approaches, fostering greater significant interactions with students whilst improving teaching effectiveness.

However, the developing integration of AI also calls for instructors to develop new skills and adapt to technological improvements. Educators need to come to be talented in the usage of AI gear, knowledge how to integrate them into their coaching practices, and interpreting the information these structures generate. The future of coaching will possibly contain a more collaborative model where instructors paintings in tandem with AI systems to beautify the studying revel in. Consequently, this evolution of roles offers both demanding situations and opportunities for educators to redefine their expert identities.

AI-supported coaching performs a pivotal role in team of workers training and upskilling. As industries face fast technological changes, employees are required to continuously update their abilities to live aggressive. AI structures are an increasing number of getting used to facilitate lifelong mastering, providing people with access to personalized training applications tailor-made to their person wishes and career dreams.

For instance, AI-powered platforms can analyze an employee's cutting-edge ability set and advocate tailor-made studying paths to assist them collect new talents or increase of their careers. These structures can also alter training programs based on a learner's development, making sure that individuals obtain the suitable challenges and assist to satisfy their targets. This personalised, flexible method to training guarantees that employees are geared up to navigate the evolving job marketplace, whether or not it entails adopting new technology, enhancing leadership skills, or gaining knowledge of complex hassle-fixing strategies.

AI also helps agencies in personnel improvement by means of imparting data-driven insights into worker overall performance. By tracking development and figuring out know-how gaps, AI enables agencies to make knowledgeable choices approximately schooling investments, ensuring that sources are allotted efficaciously to assist both person and organizational growth.

Despite the various benefits AI offers in transforming schooling and the staff, it additionally offers several demanding situations. One key problem is the capacity displacement of jobs, in particular the ones concerning repetitive duties that may be automated via AI. For example, administrative obligations in instructional settings, including scheduling and grading, can be fully automatic, reducing the demand for sure assist workforce positions.

In addition to process displacement, there are worries regarding information privacy and security in AI-supported academic environments. AI structures gather sizeable amounts of statistics about college students' gaining knowledge of patterns and overall performance, elevating questions about how this records is controlled and who has get admission to to it. Educational establishments, teachers, and students must be aware of these risks and take steps to make sure that private information is included from unauthorized get admission to.

Another task lies inside the capacity for widening the skills gap. As AI technology will become extra advanced, there will be a more want for employees who possess specialized understanding in fields together with AI improvement, facts science, and gadget mastering. However, the supply of education in those regions may not be equally reachable to all people. This can cause disparities within the staff, with a few workers gaining a competitive area while others are left behind. To cope with this mission, academic systems and employers must prioritize presenting equitable access to AI-related education and assets to make certain that each one people have the opportunity to thrive in a rapidly changing process marketplace.

AI-supported teaching is reshaping both schooling and the workforce by means of enabling personalised learning reports and improving coaching efficiency. While it offers great benefits in phrases of preparing college students for the destiny job market, it additionally offers challenges, in particular in phrases of staff displacement, information security, and access to specialised education. The destiny of training and paintings will depend on how properly society adapts to these adjustments, integrating AI into coaching while making sure that the staff remains agile, professional, and ready for the demands of the digital financial system.

7.3 Investment in Education and Technological Infrastructure

As the demand for AI integration into education rises, so does the need for significant investment in technological infrastructure. To create an environment where AI can truly transform education, educational institutions, governments, and private sectors must commit to developing the necessary technological foundation. This infrastructure includes high-speed internet access, cloud computing, data storage solutions, and AI software platforms.

The challenge lies in ensuring that these technologies are not only available but also accessible to all students, regardless of their geographic location or economic background. Investing in technology infrastructure will bridge the digital divide, ensuring that even underserved communities and institutions can benefit from the advances AI offers. This will require a strategic focus on making education technology more affordable and scalable while continuing to innovate in software development and hardware design.

Moreover, educational institutions must be prepared to constantly update their technological resources. AI technologies are rapidly evolving, and to remain competitive, educational systems need to stay ahead of the curve by continuously investing in the latest tools and software that can deliver effective, personalized learning experiences.

While technological infrastructure is essential, funding for AI-driven education programs also plays a pivotal role in fostering innovation in the field. Governments, private companies, and philanthropic organizations need to invest in research and development (R&D) to create AI models specifically designed for educational purposes. This investment ensures the development of tools that meet the diverse needs of learners and teachers.

Additionally, funding is necessary for pilot programs that test AI technologies in real-world educational settings. These programs can serve as testing grounds for AI's potential impact, helping educators and policymakers understand what works, what doesn't, and where further innovation is needed. By investing in these programs, stakeholders can help pave the way for widespread adoption of AI in education.

It is also important to allocate funds to train teachers and administrators on how to use AI technologies effectively. This requires investment in professional development and continuous learning opportunities that equip educators with the necessary skills to navigate the evolving landscape of AI-supported teaching. Training programs will ensure that teachers are not only users of technology but active participants in the development and integration of AI tools into the curriculum.

Building a robust technological infrastructure for AI in education cannot rely solely on public or private sectors alone. Collaboration between both is crucial to ensure sustainable progress. Public-private partnerships can enable institutions to leverage expertise, funding, and innovation in ways that benefit all stakeholders.

Governments can provide funding for large-scale technology infrastructure projects and policy initiatives that promote the integration of AI into educational systems. On the other hand, private sector companies, especially tech firms, bring the technical know-how and cutting-edge AI solutions that can drive the implementation process. For instance, partnerships with major tech companies can give educational institutions access to AI tools, such as learning management systems, that are already proven to work effectively.

Moreover, these collaborations can address important issues like access to technology in developing regions. Private sector companies can support initiatives that provide schools in underserved areas with the necessary hardware, software, and training, ensuring that AI technologies are available to all students and educators, regardless of their socio-economic background.

While immediate investments are essential for integrating AI into education, long-term sustainability is equally important. The rapid pace of technological change means that investments made today could become outdated within a few years unless continuous investment is made in keeping systems updated and relevant.

To ensure sustainability, educational institutions must create a long-term strategy that accounts for the future evolution of AI technologies. This includes setting aside funds for regular system upgrades, adopting a model of continuous improvement, and fostering an environment that encourages innovation and adaptation. Educational systems must also consider the total cost of ownership of AI technologies, which includes maintenance, updates, and the integration of new features over time.

Furthermore, there must be ongoing investment in data security and privacy protections as part of the technological infrastructure. With the increasing use of AI systems that collect and analyze student data, ensuring the safety and confidentiality of this information is paramount. Institutions must invest in robust cybersecurity measures, encryption technologies, and compliance with data protection laws to safeguard against data breaches and unauthorized access.

Investment in education technology and infrastructure is critical to unlocking the full potential of AI in education. Governments, private companies, and educational institutions must work together to build and maintain the technological infrastructure needed to support AI-driven learning. This includes providing funding for AI research and development, supporting teacher training, and ensuring long-term sustainability. By making these investments, stakeholders can create an educational ecosystem that is not only more efficient but also more inclusive and accessible, helping prepare students for the challenges of the future job market.

7.4. Funding Models for AI Integration in Education

The integration of Artificial Intelligence (AI) into training holds transformative promise, allowing personalized studying, efficient management, and expanded accessibility. However, deploying AI technology at scale calls for good sized and sustainable funding. Securing and managing those monetary resources is a complicated mission, related to various stakeholders, competing priorities, and ranging capacities across areas and institutions.

Historically, training investment has been predominantly sourced from public budgets, supplemented by way of private contributions, philanthropic grants, and tuition charges. The introduction of AI introduces new fee systems, which include fees on hardware infrastructure, software program licenses, facts control, employees training, and ongoing preservation.

These expenses may be prohibitive, mainly for underneath-resourced faculties and developing countries, necessitating diverse and flexible funding mechanisms.

One accepted model is authorities-led funding, wherein countrywide or nearby authorities allocate dedicated budgets to promote AI adoption in public schooling systems. Governments may additionally establish innovation finances, pilot programs, or countrywide AI strategies that prioritize education. This centralized method allows coordinated deployment, standardization, and equitable distribution of assets. Moreover, public funding often signals political commitment and encourages private quarter participation. However, bureaucratic constraints, competing priorities, and price range boundaries can sluggish implementation and restrict responsiveness to local wishes.

Public-non-public partnerships (PPPs) have emerged as a powerful automobile for investment AI in schooling. In PPP arrangements, governments collaborate with technology businesses, startups, and philanthropic corporations to co-expand and finance AI tasks. These partnerships leverage personal area know-how, innovation capability, and economic resources, at the same time as aligning with public training desires. For instance, era companies can also offer AI systems at discounted fees or in-type guide, while governments contribute infrastructure and regulatory frameworks. PPPs can boost up AI integration but require transparent governance structures to stability income reasons with educational equity and ethics.

Another developing road is philanthropic and nonprofit investment, where foundations and worldwide businesses invest in AI projects aimed at improving training get right of entry to and exceptional globally. Grants from entities consisting of the Gates Foundation, UNESCO, and the World Bank often target underserved populations, supporting pilot packages, capability-constructing, and research. These finances can catalyze innovation and highlight scalable first-rate practices however are typically time-confined and reliant on moving donor priorities.

Subscription and licensing fashions constitute the commercial approach to funding AI tools in education. Educational institutions or novices pay for access to AI-powered structures, software program, or offerings, frequently on a according to-consumer or per-institution basis. While this version supports ongoing software program development and preservation, it dangers except low-income faculties or students unable to manage to pay for costs, doubtlessly exacerbating instructional inequities. To mitigate this, tiered pricing, freemium models, or institutional subsidies may be hired.

Emerging fashions additionally explore crowdfunding and network financing, where educators, mother and father, and nearby stakeholders make a contribution financially to assist AI adoption in their schools. While generally modest in scale, these grassroots efforts can foster network ownership and make sure that AI tools align carefully with local academic priorities.

The rise of outcome-based investment or impact making an investment introduces performance-related financing mechanisms. In this model, buyers provide upfront capital for AI academic tasks, with returns contingent on reaching predefined academic results, such as stepped forward literacy rates or pupil engagement. This approach aligns incentives around effectiveness and innovation but requires robust metrics and obvious evaluation frameworks.

To maintain investment through the years, capacity-building and schooling investments are essential. Equipping educators and directors with AI literacy and technical talents ensures that economic assets translate into effective implementation. Governments and funders an increasing number of understand that investment in human capital is as essential as generation procurement.

Additionally, open-source and collaborative improvement fashions can reduce costs and beautify accessibility. By pooling resources and information, educational institutions and developers create AI equipment that are freely available, customizable, and adaptable to diverse contexts. Funding such projects frequently is predicated on combined fashions including presents, donations, and institutional contributions.

Finally, equitable AI integration needs focused investment to bridge digital divides. Investments in infrastructure, broadband get admission to, and tool provision are conditions for AI adoption, mainly in rural or marginalized communities. Without such foundational guide, AI's benefits hazard being concentrated amongst already advantaged groups.

Effective investment for AI integration in schooling requires a multifaceted approach that balances public obligation, personal innovation, philanthropic generosity, and network engagement. Transparent governance, fairness-targeted allocation, and ongoing assessment are important to maximizing the impact of monetary investments. By adopting diverse and sustainable funding models, stakeholders can make sure that AI technology make a contribution meaningfully to inclusive, fantastic education for all beginners.

CHAPTER 8

AI-Powered Education in the Future

8.1 The Future of Smart Educational Technologies

The future of smart educational technologies lies in the continued development and integration of AI-driven systems that personalize learning and adapt to individual students' needs. These systems are expected to evolve into more sophisticated and intuitive tools capable of providing real-time feedback, assessing student performance, and recommending tailored learning paths. As AI becomes more advanced, intelligent learning systems will be able to analyze a wider range of data points, from cognitive abilities to emotional responses, in order to optimize the learning experience for each student.

In the coming years, we can expect to see a greater reliance on deep learning algorithms, which can continually refine educational content and strategies. These systems will move beyond static, pre-defined curriculum pathways and start to offer dynamic learning experiences that adjust in real-time based on the learner's progress, interests, and even challenges. This will enable students to engage with learning materials in ways that are more aligned with their personal learning styles, enhancing their retention and comprehension.

Smart educational technologies will increasingly incorporate augmented reality (AR) and virtual reality (VR) to create immersive learning experiences. These technologies have the potential to transport students to virtual environments where they can interact with content in ways that go far beyond traditional classroom settings. For example, students may be able to explore ancient civilizations, conduct complex science experiments, or practice medical procedures in virtual spaces that simulate real-world scenarios.

In the future, AR and VR, powered by AI, will offer a more seamless integration with curricula, providing contextual and experiential learning opportunities. Teachers will be able to use these technologies to enhance lessons, enabling students to better understand abstract concepts by visualizing them in 3D. This will allow for a deeper and more engaging learning experience, particularly in subjects that benefit from hands-on practice, such as history, biology, and engineering.

As AI-powered tools become more advanced, learning analytics will play a pivotal role in shaping the future of education. Predictive tools will be able to assess a student's likelihood of success or failure in a specific area and provide actionable insights for both students and educators. This will enable a more proactive approach to learning, where interventions can be made before students fall behind.

Moreover, AI-driven learning analytics will enable more precise measurements of educational outcomes. These tools will not only assess academic performance but will also track emotional, social, and behavioral aspects of learning. With this broader scope of data, educators can gain a more holistic understanding of student development, allowing for more informed decision-making and personalized educational strategies.

These predictive tools will also help identify trends and patterns at the institutional level, offering valuable insights into the effectiveness of different teaching methodologies, curricula, and technology implementations. Educational leaders will be able to make data-driven decisions that can improve the learning experience for all students and optimize the allocation of resources.

While AI will continue to evolve as a core component of smart educational technologies, the future of education will likely see a stronger collaboration between AI and human educators rather than AI replacing teachers altogether. In this future scenario, AI will support educators by automating administrative tasks, offering personalized learning tools, and providing data-driven insights, allowing teachers to focus more on fostering creativity, critical thinking, and emotional intelligence in their students.

Educators will still play a crucial role in mentoring and guiding students, offering the human connection and emotional support that AI cannot replicate. However, AI will augment their abilities by providing real-time insights into student progress, suggesting individualized resources, and helping identify areas where students need additional help. In this way,

AI will act as a powerful assistant to human teachers, enhancing their effectiveness and enabling them to meet the needs of diverse learners.

The future of AI in education is not limited to K-12 or university-level learning. AI will be instrumental in facilitating lifelong learning by providing accessible, flexible learning opportunities for adults in various stages of their careers. AI-powered platforms will offer personalized learning experiences for people seeking to develop new skills, whether for professional advancement or personal enrichment.

These platforms will offer on-demand learning tailored to the individual's schedule, pace, and preferred learning style. AI systems will also monitor and track progress, ensuring that learners stay on track to meet their goals. By leveraging AI, individuals will be able to access customized learning paths that meet their specific needs, whether they are reskilling for a new job, pursuing a hobby, or staying up-to-date with the latest industry trends.

As smart educational technologies continue to evolve, they will bring about new challenges and ethical considerations. One of the most significant concerns is ensuring that these technologies are accessible to all students, regardless of socio-economic status or geographic location. Efforts must be made to ensure that AI-powered educational tools are not only available but also affordable, so that students in underserved communities can benefit from the same opportunities as those in more privileged areas.

Moreover, privacy and data security will remain paramount concerns as AI systems collect and analyze vast amounts of student data. Schools, governments, and tech companies will need to work together to establish regulations and best practices that protect student information while still allowing AI systems to function effectively. This includes ensuring transparency in how student data is used and providing clear guidelines for data access and sharing.

The future of smart educational technologies promises to revolutionize how we learn and teach. AI-powered systems will create more personalized, adaptive, and immersive learning experiences that engage students in ways that traditional education methods cannot. By incorporating technologies such as AR, VR, and advanced learning analytics, educators will have the tools to meet the diverse needs of their students, preparing them for success in an increasingly complex and fast-changing world. However, as we move forward, it is essential to address the ethical and accessibility challenges that come with these innovations, ensuring that AI in education benefits all learners equally.

8.2 Innovative Models in Education with AI

One of the most innovative applications of AI in education is the development of adaptive learning systems. These systems use AI algorithms to continuously monitor student performance and tailor educational content to meet the learner's evolving needs. Unlike traditional one-size-fits-all educational models, adaptive learning systems provide personalized learning experiences, adjusting the pace, difficulty, and style of the material based on each student's progress and abilities.

As AI technologies evolve, adaptive learning platforms will become even more sophisticated, using machine learning to predict and respond to learning gaps, misconceptions, and challenges in real-time. By leveraging vast amounts of data, AI-driven adaptive models will provide a more targeted approach to learning, ensuring that students receive the right content at the right time. This dynamic system will optimize learning efficiency and outcomes, particularly for students who may struggle in traditional classroom settings.

For example, an AI system could identify that a student is having difficulty understanding a specific math concept and offer additional resources, such as practice problems, tutorials, or visual aids, to help the student improve. The system would then adjust the lesson plan, allowing the student to progress once mastery is achieved. This real-time adjustment of content ensures that no student falls behind and that each learner receives individualized support, regardless of their learning pace or style.

Another innovative model in education is the integration of AI with project-based learning (PBL). In traditional educational settings, PBL encourages students to engage in collaborative, real-world projects to develop critical thinking, problem-solving, and teamwork skills. AI can significantly enhance PBL by providing real-time feedback and support, helping students navigate complex projects more efficiently and effectively.

AI-powered tools can facilitate collaboration by analyzing team dynamics, identifying strengths and weaknesses, and offering personalized suggestions for group tasks. Furthermore, AI can help students manage and track their projects by recommending resources, organizing timelines, and predicting potential obstacles based on previous data. As students work on projects, AI can monitor their progress and provide adaptive feedback to guide them through the problem-solving process, enhancing their ability to work independently and creatively.

Additionally, AI can help bridge the gap between theoretical knowledge and practical application by offering simulations and virtual environments where students can test their ideas and learn through experimentation. For example, a student working on an engineering project could use AI tools to simulate real-world conditions and test the viability of their design, gaining deeper insights into the project's feasibility before implementation. By integrating AI into project-based learning, students are empowered to engage in more meaningful, hands-on learning experiences that reflect the complexities of the real world.

AI can also play a transformative role in gamification, which is becoming an increasingly popular method for engaging students in active learning. By incorporating game-like elements into education, such as scoring, rewards, and challenges, AI can make learning more interactive and enjoyable. AI-powered educational games can assess a student's progress and adapt the challenges accordingly, ensuring that they are appropriately challenged while avoiding frustration from tasks that are too difficult.

Gamified learning experiences powered by AI can be particularly beneficial in subjects like mathematics, language learning, and STEM, where students often benefit from interactive problem-solving. AI can adjust the difficulty level of challenges based on real-time performance, making the learning process more dynamic and engaging. As students advance through various stages of the game, they can earn rewards, unlock new levels, and receive immediate feedback on their progress, all of which motivate them to continue learning and improving.

Moreover, AI-enabled games can provide instant feedback on mistakes, helping students understand where they went wrong and offering suggestions for improvement. This immediate correction allows learners to quickly grasp difficult concepts and prevents the reinforcement of incorrect methods. By incorporating AI into gamification, educators can create highly engaging and effective learning environments that cater to diverse learning styles and increase student motivation.

Collaborative learning models, which focus on students working together to solve problems and share knowledge, can be greatly enhanced by AI technologies. AI can facilitate collaboration by connecting students with peers who share similar interests, learning styles, or strengths, creating a network of learners who can help each other. AI systems can also monitor group interactions, assess contributions, and provide feedback on team dynamics, ensuring that each student is actively engaged and learning effectively.

Furthermore, AI can support peer feedback by analyzing students' work and offering suggestions for improvement. For example, an AI system could assess a student's essay and highlight areas for improvement, such as grammar, structure, or argumentation, before the student shares it with their peers. This allows students to focus on providing constructive, high-quality feedback rather than spending time on minor issues that can be easily corrected by AI. In turn, students can refine their work, incorporate peer suggestions, and improve their overall learning experience.

Additionally, AI-powered platforms can enable asynchronous collaboration, where students from different locations and time zones can work together on projects, share resources, and offer feedback without being constrained by geographical or temporal limitations. This fosters a global learning community that can promote cross-cultural understanding and the exchange of ideas, preparing students for a globalized world.

As AI continues to advance, we may see the development of fully autonomous learning environments, where students can learn independently with minimal intervention from human instructors. These environments would use AI to guide students through the learning process, offering tailored resources, assessments, and feedback without the need for constant teacher involvement.

In an autonomous learning environment, AI would manage the pacing, structure, and content delivery, adjusting to the individual needs of each student in real-time. Students could engage with interactive lessons, participate in virtual classrooms, and receive personalized recommendations for further learning. AI would also continuously track progress, ensuring that students remain on track to meet their learning goals.

While autonomous learning environments could provide unprecedented flexibility, they would require careful implementation to ensure that students are not left behind or isolated. AI would need to be designed to provide emotional and social support, fostering a sense of connection and engagement despite the absence of a traditional classroom setting. Additionally, students would still benefit from periodic human interaction, whether through mentorship, collaborative projects, or occasional face-to-face sessions, ensuring a balanced approach to learning.

Innovative models of education powered by AI have the potential to transform the learning experience in profound ways. From adaptive learning systems that personalize content to AI-enhanced project-based learning, gamification, and collaborative models, AI can create more engaging, efficient, and effective educational experiences. These technologies not only support individual learners but also foster collaboration and peer learning, preparing students for success in an interconnected, rapidly changing world. However, as these models evolve, it is important to balance the power of AI with the need for human connection, ensuring that technology enhances rather than replaces the human elements of education.

8.3 AI and Human Teachers in Education: Collaboration for the Future

Despite the rapid advancements in AI, the role of human teachers remains crucial in shaping the educational experience. AI can serve as an incredibly powerful tool in supporting and enhancing the teaching process, but it is unlikely to replace human educators altogether. Instead, the future of education will likely be characterized by collaboration between AI systems and human teachers, with each complementing the strengths of the other.

Human teachers bring empathy, creativity, and critical thinking to the classroom, qualities that AI, no matter how advanced, cannot replicate. Teachers are also able to understand the emotional and social dynamics of students, providing guidance and mentorship that fosters personal growth. The human touch in education is irreplaceable when it comes to building relationships, fostering social skills, and guiding students through complex moral and ethical discussions. These are areas where AI can provide data and support but cannot fully replace the nuanced understanding that a human teacher can offer.

In an AI-enhanced classroom, teachers will likely take on a more strategic role as facilitators of learning, guiding students through personalized learning paths, interpreting AI-generated insights, and providing the emotional and intellectual support that encourages motivation and perseverance. Teachers will leverage AI tools to identify learning gaps, track progress, and adapt content to suit each student's unique needs. By freeing teachers from administrative tasks, AI will enable them to focus more on the intellectual and social aspects of teaching.

In the collaborative future of education, AI will also serve as a personal assistant to teachers, providing them with powerful insights and real-time data about their students' progress. AI systems can analyze large volumes of student data and generate personalized reports, highlighting areas where students are excelling or struggling. This allows teachers to focus their efforts on students who require additional support while recognizing and celebrating individual accomplishments.

AI can also assist with administrative tasks such as grading, lesson planning, and scheduling. For example, AI tools can automatically grade multiple-choice tests, essays, or even projects, providing teachers with more time to focus on delivering high-quality lessons and interacting with students. AI-powered analytics can identify trends in student performance, enabling teachers to make data-driven decisions about how to adjust their teaching methods and strategies.

Additionally, AI tools can help teachers stay up to date with the latest developments in education by suggesting new resources, teaching methods, and tools that align with their curriculum. This allows educators to continuously refine their approaches and ensure that they are providing the best possible learning experience for their students.

The collaboration between AI and human teachers will not be without its challenges. One of the key issues will be finding the right balance between technology and human interaction. Over-reliance on AI in the classroom could lead to the loss of valuable human connection, and students may miss out on the social and emotional learning that comes from interacting with a teacher and peers.

For AI to truly complement human teaching, it must be used thoughtfully and strategically. Rather than replacing teachers, AI should serve as a tool that supports and enhances their efforts. For example, AI can handle repetitive tasks such as grading or providing instant feedback on assignments, while teachers focus on fostering critical thinking, creativity, and collaboration. This allows teachers to devote more time to individualized instruction, mentorship, and emotional support.

Additionally, the implementation of AI in classrooms must be done in a way that promotes inclusivity and diversity. AI tools should be designed to accommodate the needs of all students, including those with disabilities, language barriers, or other challenges. Teachers can play a critical role in ensuring that AI is used in a way that benefits all students and that no one is left behind.

To fully realize the potential of AI in the classroom, teachers must be properly trained in how to integrate these tools into their teaching practices. Professional development programs will be essential in equipping educators with the knowledge and skills needed to effectively use AI systems. This includes understanding the capabilities and limitations of AI, interpreting data and insights provided by AI tools, and using AI to personalize instruction and create more engaging learning experiences.

Teachers must also be trained to recognize when AI is not the appropriate solution and when human intervention is necessary. While AI can provide valuable insights, it is important to understand that it is not a replacement for human judgment, intuition, and creativity. Teachers will need to develop a critical understanding of AI and its potential impacts on education, as well as how to use these tools ethically and responsibly.

In addition to training teachers in AI technologies, educational institutions should foster a culture of collaboration and openness to innovation. Teachers should be encouraged to experiment with AI tools and share their experiences and insights with their colleagues. By creating a supportive environment for AI integration, schools can ensure that teachers feel empowered to explore new ways of teaching and learning.

Looking toward the future, the collaboration between AI and human teachers will continue to evolve. As AI systems become more advanced, they will play an even larger role in supporting personalized learning, tracking student progress, and providing feedback. However, the role of the teacher will remain indispensable. Teachers will continue to be the emotional and intellectual guides who inspire, mentor, and foster the social and cognitive development of students.

The future of education will be characterized by a more dynamic and flexible learning environment, where AI and human teachers work together to meet the diverse needs of students. This collaboration will allow for more personalized, efficient, and engaging learning experiences, ultimately helping students reach their full potential.

Ultimately, the partnership between AI and human educators will enable a more holistic and inclusive educational experience, where technology enhances the learning process, but the human connection remains at the heart of education. By combining the best of both worlds—AI's capabilities and the irreplaceable qualities of human teaching—educators will be able to create learning environments that empower students to thrive in an increasingly complex and interconnected world.

8.4. Predictive Analytics and Future Educational Trends

Predictive analytics is swiftly becoming a cornerstone within the evolution of education, supplying unprecedented possibilities to assume pupil wishes, optimize studying consequences, and inform policy selections. By leveraging sizeable datasets, state-of-the-art algorithms, and device learning strategies, predictive analytics enables educators and institutions to transport from reactive to proactive strategies, shaping the destiny trajectory of tutorial systems worldwide.

At its center, predictive analytics involves amassing and reading historic and real-time records to forecast destiny events or behaviors. In schooling, this means using data which includes attendance records, assessment scores, engagement metrics, and socio-demographic statistics to perceive styles and predict effects like scholar performance, dropout chance, or getting to know alternatives. These insights empower educators to tailor interventions, allocate assets efficiently, and design curricula that better meet learner wishes.

One of the maximum instant packages of predictive analytics is in early warning systems that perceive college students at risk of falling behind or dropping out. By reading multiple elements—which include grades, participation, and behavioral signs—AI fashions can flag beginners who require extra aid nicely earlier than problems become crucial. This early detection allows for well timed, focused interventions such as tutoring, counseling, or parental engagement, thereby enhancing retention prices and educational achievement.

Predictive analytics also informs personalized mastering pathways. By expertise how one of a kind college students reply to academic strategies and content, AI structures can forecast the only mastering sequences and modalities for person rookies. This customization complements engagement, quickens mastery, and fosters motivation, helping a shift from standardized training in the direction of more adaptive, learner-focused models.

At the institutional level, predictive analytics supports strategic making plans and aid optimization. Schools and universities can forecast enrollment developments, direction demand, and staffing desires, permitting extra green budgeting and scheduling. Moreover, studying alumni effects and hard work marketplace statistics helps align instructional services with evolving personnel requirements, ensuring graduates possess applicable capabilities.

The integration of social-emotional mastering (SEL) metrics into predictive models is an emerging fashion that broadens the scope of analytics past academic overall performance. By monitoring signs related to intellectual fitness, social engagement, and emotional properly-being, AI gear can predict college students' socio-emotional challenges and guide supportive measures. This holistic method acknowledges that learning is deeply intertwined with emotional and psychological factors.

Despite its promise, using predictive analytics in education raises vast ethical and sensible concerns. The accuracy of predictions relies upon at the exceptional and representativeness of records; biases in datasets can cause unfair or discriminatory results. Transparency about how models make predictions and how selections are derived is crucial to maintain trust among college students, parents, and educators. Additionally, safeguarding pupil privacy and statistics protection is paramount, requiring robust policies and regulatory compliance.

Another assignment is the danger of self-pleasant prophecies, where students categorized as "at threat" may also internalize these assessments, probably undermining their motivation and shallowness. Educators should consequently stability records-driven insights with human judgment and empathy, ensuring that predictive analytics serves as a tool for empowerment instead of problem.

Looking ahead, the convergence of predictive analytics with other rising technologies which include herbal language processing, virtual truth, and adaptive studying systems will create increasingly state-of-the-art academic environments. These incorporated structures will now not only forecast studying trajectories but additionally simulate personalized experiences and provide real-time modifications, making training extra dynamic and responsive.

Moreover, predictive analytics is poised to steer policy and fairness initiatives by way of highlighting systemic disparities and uncovering hidden patterns related to get entry to and outcomes. Policymakers can use those insights to layout centered programs that address achievement gaps and promote inclusive education.

Predictive analytics represents a transformative pressure within the future of training. By permitting foresight into pupil needs, institutional dynamics, and broader societal tendencies, it empowers stakeholders to make informed decisions that decorate learning studies and consequences. To fully realise its potential, predictive analytics have to be applied thoughtfully, with interest to ethics, fairness, and human-targeted values. When harnessed responsibly, it is going to be a important catalyst in shaping adaptive, effective, and equitable academic futures.

www.ingramcontent.com/pod-product-compliance
Lightning Source LLC
La Vergne TN
LVHW052058060326
832903LV00061B/3356